TURNER

SELF-PORTRAIT
Circa 1798.   Oil on canvas, 74.5 x 58.5 cm.
Tate Gallery, London.

TURNER

GUY WEELEN

TIGER BOOKS INTERNATIONAL
LONDON

*"Of **genuis** I shall speak with reserve, for no word has been more indiscriminately confounded; by genius I mean that power which enlarges the circle of human knowledge; which discovers new materials of nature, or combines the known with novelty, whilst **talent** arranges, cultivates, polishes the discoveries of genius."*

*"...The term **invention** never ought to be so misconstrued as to be confounded with that of **creation**, imcompatible with our notions of limited being, an idea of pure astonishment, and admissible only when we mention Omnipotence. To **invent** is to find; to find something presupposes its existence somewhere, implicitly, scattered or in a mass..."*

*"When the object [of the arts] is to subordinate the vehicle, whatever it be, to the real object, and make sense the minister of the mind,...**design**, in its most extensive, as in its strictest sense, is their basis; when they stoop to be the mere playthings, or debase themselves to be the debauchers of the senses, they make **colour** their insidious foundation."*

*"If the principle which animates art, gives rights and privilege to colour not its own;...if what is claimed in vain by form and mind, it fondly grants to colour;...then art is degraded to a mere vehicle of sensual pleasure, an implement of luxury, a beautiful **but trifling** bauble, or a splendid fault."*

Henry Fuseli

Translation by I. Mark Paris

This edition published in 1992 by
Tiger Books International PLC,
London

© 1981 by Nouvelles Editions Francaises Paris

English translation Copyright by Alpine Fine Arts
Collection, Ltd.

Published by special arrangement with William
S. Konecky Associates, Inc.

Designed and produced with the collaboration of Elaine
and Roger Allegret.

ISBN: 1-85501-241-3

Printed and Bound in China

JOSEPH MALLORD WILLIAM TURNER

The three European countries on which romanticism left its mark were, in probable order of its appearance, England, Germany, and France. In each case, the development of this philosophical and artistic phenomenon was molded by particularly historical and geographic circumstances; different forms emerged within each national context. No sooner do we pinpoint a characteristic feature than a disparity or variation of one kind of another—indeed a multitude of diverse individuals—comes into view. Only fourteen years separate Wordsworth and Coleridge's *Lyrical Ballads* (1798) from the meteoric success of Cantos I and II of Byron's *Childe Harold* (1812). Yet, by what common denominator are we to gauge the first generation of romantic thought as embodied in Wordsworth's works, and the full-blown romanticism of a poet like Byron?

To escape the hollow values of culture and society, Wordsworth plunged into meditation and attuned himself to murmuring water, the wind rustling in the tall grass, the voices of humble folk. He let his feelings freely radiate from within, and through that outpouring of emotion he discovered an openness, a spiritual fervor, an idealism which he held out as a model and pledge of a harmony to come. The clubfooted Byron, on the other hand, spurred by his *deamon*, hurled defiance and disdain at a society he abhorred; he could never get his fill of luxury and licentiousness to conceal from himself his insatiable need for tenderness. Wordsworth believed in man and proposed a republic of humankind, whereas the thin-skinned Byron reviled, repudiated, lashed out against his fellow man in an attempt to destroy man and himself in the process.

The philosophy of Jean-Jacques Rousseau had considerable impact on young people in England during the last decade of the eighteenth century. There his theories and fervent convictions touched off lasting and far–reaching repercussions. But English romanticism actually traced its roots to a mixture of nationalism, history and legend. Contrary to the general pattern in other countries, there was no body of theoretical writings to back up and elucidate this new surge of feeling and passion. Nor did English writers form a coherent group, even if one can point to the philosophical compatibility of, say, Wordsworth and Coleridge, or Shelley and Keats, or Byron and Shelley. Moreover, poets and painters, albeit stars within one and the same constellation, moved in different worlds. Byron never spoke of Turner, and Wordsworth did not know the first thing about his painting (although we should bear in mind that Turner's overtly romantic phase blossomed too late for Byron, and his dramatic, violent subjects had nothing whatever in common with Wordsworthian concerns).

The Napoleonic wars had left Europe devastated. After the demise of the emperor and his absurd dream, people had no choice but to muster their strength and pick up the pieces. Industrialization, which had been underway in England since the beginning of the eighteenth century, provided the wealthy and educated with a whole new field of endeavor on which to practice their spirit of enterprise. Order and morality were duly requisitioned to serve as the handmaidens of business and the burgeoning world of money matters. ''From then on, there were two camps,'' wrote Alfred de Musset. ''On one side, all the effusive, uplifted souls who hankered after the infinite. Amid tears and great suffering, they bowed their heads and enveloped themselves in morbid dreaming; there was nothing left but fragile reeds on an ocean of bitterness. On the other side, all the worldly ones who stood erect and unbending in a sea of material pleasures. All they cared about was counting the money they had amassed. There was nothing but a sob and a burst of laughter—one from the soul, the other from the body.''

In a splendid book on romanticism in painting, Jean Clay scanned the movement in all its teeming diversity and attempted to sift through the resources which English, German and French artists drew on. In the three spheres of endeavor that were destined to produce masterpieces—literature, music, and painting—romanticism expressed itself in an infinite variety of ways, and all too often the shape it assumed was ill–defined. But the spirit of romanticism, the yearnings and aspirations which underlie its diverse and sometimes contradictory forms, are less difficult to pinpoint.

First, it may be said that the twofold aim of romanticism was to shatter and confuse everything which so–called classical thought had endeavored to segregate and clarify. It reflected an irrepressible, often enraged need to sever ties with a society that for too long had borne the yoke of rationalist assumptions. It was the body's turn to get even; the time had come to flout the tyrannical laws imposed by convention and morality. It was a burning desire for freedom, a stormy insistence on an individual's right to pit himself against death, now perceived as something one chose, not awaited. Oscillating between freedom and fate, the romantic unfurled his cape, unsheathed his glittering sword, and gave full rein to the shadowy steeds of his imagination. At the same time, he was secretly aware that the undertaking was doomed to failure, and this made his ordeal that much more bitter or desperate. He was caught in a trap, so he struggled; but it was last, futile burst of energy before the end.

Was it a genuine battle or just so much gesticulation, just so much playacting? The dishonest ones were those who did it for show, for "action on stage is life lived indirectly, at a distance" (Jean-Jacques Mayoux). In any event, it was not long before the romantic imagination, aroused by the idylls and exploits of Olympian gods, then of dashing heroes, waxed ironic and held up both to ridicule. An overdose of sublime had triggered a turnabout in values. The poets and writers cleared the way for the painters, who, after 1830, got caught up in the act. Clowns from England, tumblers, cavorting riders—these were their new stars. "When the circus and its illusions are presented as the arena of truth," wrote Jean Starobinski, "what is left of the academic tradition of the great and the beautiful?"

A number of them heeded the enigmatic call of death: Shelley perished at the hand of Fate (the shipwreck is still considered an accident); Byron, consumed with fever in the marshlands of Greece, died for freedom's sake; Hölderin pursued his poetic ideal in the maze of madness; Nerval, whose "star-spangled lute [bore] the black sun of melancholy," succumbed to despair. And, if I may be so bold as to add this name, there was van Gogh, that romantic lost in time, who wanted to "express terrible human passions with red and green": his mind gave way under the strain of the public's obtuseness. The list is far from complete, for romanticism is a *modus vivendi* of humankind.

"Words are the image, not of things, but of the person uttering them," writes Tzvetan Todorov. In our desire to communicate, we are the victims of the limits imposed by definitions, and even more, of the way we express ourselves. Since the beginning of time, body and mind have been locked in a ruthless battle that pits violence against order. Probably it does not lie with man to strike a balance between the two. Order and violence: in the course of history—or of a single lifetime—societies and individuals have grasped now one weapon, now the other. The struggle remains undecided; neither side has yet emerged victorious. Anything won or achieved is temporary. Even works of art are subject to constant reappraisal. They, too, can perish; but they can be reborn. Such works are understood only to those who are inclined to see themselves in them. Each time this act of self-recognition occurs, they flash up again for an instant, then grow dim or die out. Nowadays, the deeply-ingrained frame of mind once known as romanticism is called Surrealism. It, too, emerged from the horrors of war.

The sad and disenchanting fact is that we go on and on playing the same game with the same deck of marked cards. In the final analysis, all that matters is how our defeat is to be concealed beneath colors or amid sounds.

Joseph Mallord William Turner was both a great poet and a great painter. Oscar Wilde used to say something to the effect that great poets put their poetry into their work, unimportant ones put their poetry into their lives. Fortunately for art, Turner put his poetry into his painting. Unfortunately for Turner, his life seems to have been anything but poetic, and the same could be said about his poem, *The Fallacies of Hope.*

Homely and shabbily dressed, Turner spent a deprived childhood caught between a submissive father and an ill-tempered mother who was subject to tantrums. Circumstances must have often compelled the child to hide his feelings (or himself) in order to escape the stormy aftermath of her outbursts. Humble people of modest means, the Turners worshiped at the altar of money. Thrift was the chief virtue of these shopkeepers who naively marveled at titles, social status, and success. They were duly obsequious to their customers and to the privileged few who had the gold they were so eager to get their hands on.

As his mother's fits degenerated into madness, it was decided that she should be shut away where no one could see her. Father and son did their utmost to put her out of their minds—a strategy which, when not successfully carried through, did its share of damage. Her presence weighed that much more heavily upon young Turner for her not being there; he longed for her all the more. Joseph was all of eleven when his little sister, Mary Ann, died. Another absence, another rent in the fabric of his emotions. Once again the lad felt disconsolate and forlorn.

His well-intentioned parents sent him away from the bereaved family home just after the death of his little playmate. And so he bore his burden of sorrow alone, far from his loved ones. Whether a person shows stamina in adversity, or succumbs to it, is more a matter of disposition than of will. We have no way of determining which outlook Turner adopted. To be sure, people have drawn their own conclusions after the fact, but it is all conjecture. Turner was tight-lipped when it came to divulging information about his attitudes and moods: his biography had to be reconstructed after his death. But even if we heard it from his own lips, would such statements be any more believable than those made by his friends or by Ruskin, his most ardent admirer?

When asked by Ruskin to recall her impressions of Turner, Ann Dart obliged with the following portrait: "[Turner] was not like young people in general, he was singular and very silent, seemed exclusively devoted to his drawing....He seemed an uneducated youth, desirous of nothing but improvement in his art.'' Clara Wheeler, the daughter of Turner's close friend William Frederick Wells, cast the artist in quite a different light. ''Of all the light-hearted, merry creatures I ever knew, Turner was the most so; and the laughter and fun that abounded when he was an inmate of our cottage was inconceivable.'' After his first interview with his ''man of genius,'' Ruskin wrote: ''Everybody had described him to me as coarse, boorish, unintellectual, vulgar. This I knew to be impossible. I found in him a somewhat eccentric, keen-mannered, matter-of-fact; English-minded gentleman; good-natured evidently, bad-tempered evidently, hating humbug of all sorts, shrewd, perhaps a little selfish, highly intellectual, the powers of the mind not brought out with any delight in their manifestation, or intention of display...'' The finishing touch to this thumbnail sketch comes from Clara Wheeler: ''No one would have imagined, under that rather rough and cold exterior, how very strong were the affections which lay hidden beneath.''

I should like to propose a thumbnail sketch of my own based on the wealth of facts and anecdotes gleaned from his friends and diligently passed on by his biographers. Turner was agreeable and cheerful with those whose affection he felt sure of; with others he had no time to lose and was not inclined to mask his feelings. They made him pay for his indifference and sudden changes in mood. At the same time, Turner's fierce ambition in matters concerning his art impelled him to take distasteful, even obsequious measures to ensure its success. But without this gnawing ambition, this dedication to his art, Turner would never have been the great painter he was—so enthusiastic about his craft that he ended up reinventing it. Had he not been obsessed with an art that he wanted to be the greatest of all arts, he would not have devoted his thoughts, his entire life to it as he did, to the point of removing himself from the mainstream of life. He lived in another world; he lived through and in his paintings. Every creator is self-centered, everything he creates makes demands upon him (with all due deference to the pests who would steal into that world).

The school of frugality in which Turner had been tutored left its mark on him. He knew his worth and stood up to Lord Elgin and his publishers in order to get the money he needed. If he led a Spartan existence, it was more out of indifference than stinginess.. In the end, his much-disparaged avarice was redeemed by an act of generosity. The painter left his fortune to a ''Charitable Institution....for the Maintenance and Support of Poor and Decayed Male Artists,'' although they had to be ''born in England and of English Parents only and lawful issue.'' He had learned the hard way about the tribulations that life holds in store for those not provided for, the bitter pill of an uncomprehending public, the stinging wounds of intolerance.

The silence with which he greeted reviews—no doubt he brooded over them by the fireside come evening—attested to both his vulnerability and keen self-awareness. His retorts could be sharp, often acrimonious; but when confronted with authority he knew how to champ at the bit and hold his peace. The cost of the public's obtuseness was the isolation in which the artist sought refuge toward the end of his life. In spite of everything, he clung to his inconsistent desire to be admired; he never gave up hope of being recognized. His bequest to the nation smacks of megalomania, and it was as much as anything else an act of defiance designed to foil the injustice of fate.

His recourse to alcohol and his escapades in the brothels of Margate bear witness to the intensity of his quest, the violence of his impulses. Unfortunately for Turner, however, he lived in an age when those who subscribed to Victorian morality (including Ruskin, who ruthlessly had evidence of Turner's licentiousness destroyed) looked upon such impulses as something to be ashamed of. It was impossible for Ruskin to understand that his painting might be the rechanneled, sublimated outpouring of a frustrated and victimized sexual drive. ''It will always be greater to imagine than to live,'' writes Gaston Bachelard. Those clandestine visits to Margate as his life drew to a close speak at once for his guilt, his despair, and the extent to which he had shut himself off from the world. Apparently the two or three women with whom he had relations for a while were not, like Baudelaire's dazzling mistress, the stele of his imagination. His indifference toward them indicated more an incompatibility than an annoyance, and incompatibility led to aloofness. Nor did his two illegitimate daughters, Georgianna and Evelina, provide him with the certainty that at last he might achieve some degree of lasting happiness. Could he have achieved it in any event? Had he been able, would he have chosen to do so?

So ingrained was Turner's tendency to dissemble that one might go so far as to say that he had a kind of split personality. In his case, hiding was simply a matter of habit. He kept his distance and finally had to hide to elude the tantrums of an unbalanced mother. Sometimes he had to be quick to parry just to ensure his own safety. He joined in the family's silence surrounding her confinement and her memory. Her death was buried in oblivion. How strongly her presence must have been felt, to have had to bury her twice! His father was kept in the background and looked for all the world like a manservant. Of course, Turner could rationalize by believing that it saved him the cost of an assistant—and rationalize he did.

He publicly exhibited most of his works at the Royal Academy or in his gallery, but some he kept secret, that is, out of sight. The task of distinguishing the so-called finished paintings from those considered ''unfinished''

Varley: Turner
(1815–1820)

Hardraw Fall (c. 1816–1818)

turned out to be a game of hide-and-seek. Were the "unfinished" paintings in fact finished? Vice-Chancellor Kindersley cut the game short by refusing to go on making the distinction. There was something about those paintings which Turner had squirreled away that had caught his attention. Given the way people's taste and thinking have evolved, they are now acclaimed as the most compelling and mysterious works in the Turner oeuvre, the ones in which, as Laurence Binyon put it, "he seems to take the light itself upon his brush." Today we shudder to think that they might have been destroyed or left to rot. When Reverend Trimmer's son finally paid a visit to Turner's studio after the artist's death, he felt as thought he had entered a "shrine" to which no one before him had ever been privy.

In the official version of Turner's life, he was the only character in a one-man play. He concealed his personal relationships or quite simply pretended that people like Sarah Danby or Sophia Carolyn Booth were not a part of his life. In a letter to James Holworthy (December, 1826), he wrote that "I am a kind of slave who puts on his own fetters from habit, or more like what my Derbyshire friends would say, an Old Batchelor who puts his coat on always one way,"; a flash of lucidity quickly glossed over by a touch of self-mockery. The mysterious lady from Jersey, known to us by a very sketchy letter, was part of Thornbury's simplistic thinking on the matter. When he finally withdrew to Margate, he went about incognito—as Sophia Carolyn Booth! It must have been all too obvious to shopkeepers and customers in pubs and elsewhere that he was hiding under an assumed named. He would sometimes go to even greater lengths to avoid recognition by pretending to be a captain or an admiral.

No doubt keeping up this disguise was a shrewd and ticklish business that called for an arsenal of carefully worked-out ruses and precautionary measures—all of which attests to his burning desire to hide. All of his biographers, Finberg in particular, have interpreted this as nothing more than a wish to be left in peace, a simple enough wish that the artist found difficult to fulfill. Might not this right to peace and quiet have been the first stage in a longer–indeed, eternal—repose? Might it not have been his way of expressing a hidden desire to "play dead," as the popular expression goes for people who want to drop out of sight? At the end of his life, he succeeded in doing just that. To make people forget he existed even though he was still alive, even though he had once forgotten his own mother, even though he had struggled *not* to be forgotten—how overpowering is the need to hide, since it is a need to hide oneself.

Artists do not live the way they create, and this is especially true of Turner. It ought to be put the other way around: artists create the way they live deep within themselves. In a series of superb books, Gaston Bachelard took great pains to show that the images produced within a poet's imagination are extensions of his dream world. His preferred field of inquiry was poetic imagery, not painted images; the former does lend itself more readily to analysis than the latter. But how can one look at a painting and not see in it an imagination hard at work? Since it so happens that most of Turner's paintings are accompanied by literary notations, someone ought to undertake a three-pronged study *à la Bachelard*, one that examines the images in the paintings, those in Turner's often fastidious titles, and those in the accompanying lines of verse (1).

To see is, if not actually to possess, then at least to catch or hold for a while. The eye must come to grips with harshness, violence, fear, and sadism. True, sublimation is always possible: witness the pink–and–azure seraphic visions of Fra Angelico. The images an artist selects from among all those the world offers him are significant simply for their having been chosen. Returning time and again to a form which fits effortlessly into a composition or proves essential to its structure, one which reappears each time in a different guise—such forms, stylistically speaking, are anything but bad habits that take up where inventiveness leaves off. In a way, they are as illuminating as a slip of the tongue, for they too reveal what is supposed to remain hidden.

Turner worshiped light. His entire oeuvre is an ascent toward light. In one of his earliest attempts to render its effects *(Fishermen at Sea)*, illumination is confined to an ellipse of clouds around that moon and is almost perfectly mirrored in the elipse of water whipping up around the boat. In *Caernarvon Castle*, the oval of the sun's yellow halo is picked up in the general contour of the bay. Similar in form are the glowing cumulus clouds which sweep across the seething sky in the painting incorrectly entitled *The Fifth Plague of Egypt*. A patch of bright blue punctures the lowering sky of *Calais Pier*. A glowing oval is once again the source of light amid the ravaged skies of *Snow Storm: Hannibal and His Army Crossing the Alps*, and many commentators have spoken of this shape as a "womb" of light. Both *Mortlake Terrace* and *Petworth Park: Tillington Church in the Distance* are structured around an elongated oval. The moon in *Keelmen Heaving in Coals by Moonlight* is also oval-shaped. A sweeping curve about to crystallize into the same shape can be seen in both *Norham Castle: Sunrise* and *The 'Fighting Témeraire' Tugged to Her Last Berth to be Broken Up*; it also occurs in *The Slave Ship, Snow Storm,* and *Shade and Darkness*.

(ill. 28)

(ill. 20)
(ill. 31)
(ill. 51)
(ill. 77, 73)
(ill. 109)
(ill. 151, 110)
(ill. 108, 134)

There was another oft-repeated image: the path of light, as Ruskin described it in *The Slave Ship*, a painting which he himself owned for a while. This double line, often appearing as a reflection of the sun or moon in water, crops up time and again in various forms in a great many of Turner's works. Its persistent recurrence cannot be explained away in terms of laws concerning the propagation of light. Turner was a romantic; he transformed the

(1) I have deliberately shortened the titles of paintings mentioned in the introduction.
The complete titles may be found on the flaps immediately preceding each set of illustrations.

8

world. The age of realism had not yet dawned. One may ask: is a painting's structure determined solely by that part of the mind which is ruled by logic?

The meanings of these images are not difficult to make out; they are obvious. Their continual reappearance affords us a glimpse into the rapturous emotion that held sway over Turner's poetic genius. Painting, like poetry, is reverie and therefore rich in hidden meaning.

View in the Basses Alpes (c. 1830)

Turner's attraction to mountains, so often depicted in his work in all their harshness and majesty, may have stemmed from a more general historical and cultural interest in the theme. Picturesque mountain-dwellers became quite the rage during the romantic era: ''...to me/High mountains are a feeling...,'' declared Byron in a fine display of how human nature can be projected onto Nature through poetry. Moreover, these dramatic portrayals of earth and rock appealed to a vast audience, that is, an assured source of income. In any event, Turner could hardly ignore the mania for mountains. *The Fall of an Avalanche in the Grisons (Cottage Destroyed by an Avalanche)* (ill. 47) brilliantly demonstrates his undeniable success with the theme; Ruskin went into raptures over the boulder crashing across the picture. Another example is *The Battle of Fort Rock, Val d'Aoste, Piedmont*. But Turner was not a (ill. 59) creature of the earth. It seems to me that, superbly crafted though these ''terrestrial'' works may be, they do not reveal a truly profound sympathy between Turner's imagination and his subject. One gets the same impression, for example, from many of the portraits Rembrandt was commissioned to paint.

Turner, like Shelley, was a quintessential man of the sea, of water. He did not simply describe it; he lived it in whatever form it assumed—now suffused with light, now convulsed by savage swells. He could evoke its eerie melancholy *(Sun Rising through Vapour: Fishermen Cleaning and Selling Fish)*; its ethereal sprightliness *(Regulus)*; its (ill. 32, 97) impending violence *(Staffa: Fingal's Cave)*; its enigmatic power *(The 'Fighting Téméraire' Tugged to Her Last Berth to be* (ill. 110) *Broken Up)*. He could exult in its vehemence *(Snow Storm)*. The raging sea would trigger the artist's aggressiveness (ill. 143) and work him up into a feverish state. He pitted his strength against her alongside the sailors; his violence was a response to the violence of the hand-to-hand struggle taking place around him. Storms unleashed the fury of his imagination and his hands.

Turner was fascinated by the high seas—immense, deep, unchanging, yet so volatile—but he was equally enthralled by tranquil, gleeful bodies of water studded with shimmering reflections. In the so-called unfinished paintings of his later years, water permeates every solid form. *Sunrise with a Boat between Headlands* and *Landscape* (ill. 153, 154) *with a River and a Bay in the Distance* are but two dazzling examples of glittering, iridescent mists that shatter and saturate our field of vision. For Turner, water was a subject so rich in meaning that even his undulating mountains (such as those in *Val d'Aoste)* seem to echo the rhythm of waves. Are not folds in the earth petrified, but equally fierce counterparts of waves? After all, water was the primordial element of the universe. But even if one does not subscribe to that statement, the fact remains that there is not a single castle, tree or sailboat in Turner's oeuvre that is not reflected in water.

This immense mirroring of objects was, for Turner and nature alike, rooted in narcissism. The world gazed upon itself one last time in the legendary waters of the Flood. Turner immersed himself in it, saw himself in it, discovered himself in it. He was both the contemplator and the object of his contemplation. To depict the world, painters have at their disposal a surface which calls for, and indeed warrants the wiles of perspective, but never cheap illusion. The modulating colors in *Val d'Aoste* imperceptibly blend into one another; they close in on the observer like an encroaching fog. Turner delved into the same liquid universe that was to captivate the imagination of Monet and Chagall.

An artist who would render fluidity of this sort must come to terms with a new pictorial language which has little in common with ''descriptive'' painting. Description always implies a gap between the object being described and the person doing the describing. An analytical approach brings choices and hierarchies into play, and time is their implicit accomplice. What occurred with Turner was a mystical, undoubtedly erotic, but above all elemental fusion which fostered a state of premonitory reverie. As a rule, this came about as a jolt, as an instantaneous impression.

Fire was equally capable of eliciting poetic raptures, proof that ambivalence must be included in any discussion of Turner's artistic vision. Although he had not actually witnessed the eruption of Mt. Soufrière, he decided to (ill. 35) paint the event after a single sketch drawn at the scene by a ''Hugh P. Keane, Esq.'' The cataclysm fired his imagination: ''Then in stupendous horror grew/The red volcano to the view,'' in the painting as well as to those who had seen the catastrophe. In 1819, he dropped everything and rushed to Naples to watch Vesuvius erupt. Perhaps in the recesses of his memory there lurked those other destructive outbursts he dreaded, but felt drawn to nonetheless. In 1834 he rushed to the *Burning of the House of Lords and Commons*. Caught up in the excitement of (ill. 106) the moment, he broke with custom and executed elaborate on-the-spot watercolors. The fireworks he shot over Venice in *Juliet and Her Nurse* were wholly unwarranted in terms of both composition and ''accuracy,'' an inconsistency that provoked the unforgiving remarks of Rev. John Eagles. But poetic fervor does not have to answer to

Juliet and Her Nurse (1836)

rationalist arguments. In 1840, he set his canvas ablaze with *Rockets and Blue Lights.* Turner's dream turned into reality with *The Slave Ship,* where carnage tinges the sea a fiery red, and again in the uncanny *Fire at Sea,* in which the artist's overheated imagination made it seem as if the sea itself were on fire. There are countless instances in the Turner oeuvre where the blazing sun and the heaving sea surpass in enthusiasm and conviction the mythological and the heroic. Whether gentle or intense, heat sparked within the artist a dim awareness of primordial bliss.

Turner fathomed the meaning of immensity, of boundless horizons, and knew how to depict them. Thus, an erupting volcano or a burning building stands out as a concentrated area of fire. On his canvases the sun is compressed into a glowing sphere. At times he placed it somewhere outside the picture, its power of illumination no less supreme for being concealed. Or the sun might be veiled in mist, or turn into a glaring blob of color so dense as to seem palpable. It is manifest and hidden at the same time. "More than any other element," writes Gaston Bachelard, "man's relationship with fire points up his tendency to yearn for concentrated power....It is the little taking revenge on the great, the hidden on the manifest." I shall not dwell on "the hidden taking revenge on the minifest," which we have already encountered in Turner's private life. Suffice it to say that an artist's life and his life's work are played out on one and the same turf. I shall confine myself here to "the little taking revenge on the great." Man worships fire, senses the depth of its symbolic meaning and becomes aware of his own insignificance as he contemplates it.

We know from everything he did that, for at least thirty years (by Ruskin's reckoning), Turner made every effort to comply with the rules of art prescribed by the Academy. The remarkable thing is that, except for this *Self-Portrait* (c. 1798), *Jessica,* and *Two Women with a Letter,* there are no half-length or full-length portraits in his oeuvre. On the other hand, he returned time and again to dense crowds, clusters of humanity adrift in some vast setting, whether natural, topographical, or architectural. Others before me have seen fit to dwell on this tendency, but far be it from me to give Turner's imagination sole credit for this particular handling of human proportion. My aim is simply to cull certain recurrent, and therefore significant images from all those which appear in his work, and I think there is reason to wonder at his inability to acquiesce to one of the pivotal rules of academic painting: to exalt the greatness and importance of man, using height itself as an effect if need be.

In the paintings of Claude Lorrain, man calmly takes his place amid the radiant splendor of the landscape around him. In Turner's, especially those after 1829, man seems overwhelmed, caught up in some sort of drama. Whenever he depicted mythological harmony in a tranquil Italianate setting, in accordance with academic convention, he could not refrain from charging the atmosphere with gloomy forebodings. Not that these works lack idealized figures. Leading ladies cavorting beneath garlands, leading men dressed in togas or armor, monks pronouncing curses, startled wood nymphs—all of the requisite characters are there. But Turner's anguish prompted him to demolish Caligula's palace, break up foliage into lonely clumps, depict buildings with terraces jutting out over the void or lookouts nestled high above the ground. These effects conspire to create an aura of oppression. *The Goddess of Discord* gave him the opportunity to display the scaly dragon of the dispute atop a lofty crag (not so much, as is often claimed, for moralistic as for idealistic reasons). Trees had not yet been consumed by light; they kept their lonely vigil as *obbligato* to the main components of the composition.

There can be no denying or belittling the formal beauty of these paintings. The fact remains, however, that they were Turner's chance to demonstrate his "culture" and virtuoso technique. He held his fiery imagination in abeyance and let his competitiveness come to the fore. Decked out in the reigning fashion of the day, these few paintings which sound the "approved" stock themes of antiquity heralded the tide that was to sweep over Europe during the nineteenth century. Quite often all that rose to the surface were stiff, colorless images taken from schoolroom manuals. To my knowledge, academic painters never took advantage of Turner's art. Yet, until World War I, there would be no more stream crossings, waterfalls, iris or morning-glories in the grotesque works of these bombastic artists without a plump lorette cast in the role of a callipygian Venus. The hackneyed images which countless students in academies of fine arts applied by rote account, in part, for the high standing they enjoy today in the estimation of authorities, who seem taken more with method and technique than imagination. Perhaps we ought not to dismiss it wholesale as a failure; in all fairness, some of the wreckage is worth saving. But the list of treasures floating to the surface would hardly tax the deeper levels of our imagination. We would be left with a catalogue of deliberately captivating, but cut-rate visions concocted by a society that was driven by a single passion, namely, the preservation of its powers and hierarchies: money, order, and the requisite dose of religion to be administered at one's convenience.

For some romantics, the thought of man's uncertainty and helplessness in the face of nature's hostility was a wrenching experience. One of those overwhelmed by the plight of humankind was the French poet Alfred de Vigny, who took refuge in heroic stoicism. In England, Byron thrashed about like a trapped animal. Turner, for his part, took his stand against fate during the last twenty years of his life, and although the ways in which he voiced his horror at the human condition varied, the message was always the same. *Fire at Sea, Shade and Darkness,*

Fingal's Cave, Rain, Steam, and Speed—these, among others, were frightened laments or ineffectual cries of protest. Turner's oeuvre abounds with boats, schooners, ships with colors flapping in the breeze, steel steamboats—all leaving in their wake a frothy backwash of nostalgia. Departures for far-off expeditions, to imaginary ports-of-call *(Port Ruysdael)*, towards the unknown. In these wooden hulls tossed upon a heaving sea, Turner seemed to rediscover a refuge, a rocking motion of a different king. The boats with furled sails *(The 'Fighting Téméraire')*, the sailboats *(Yacht Approaching the Coast)*, the weary, ungainly barks—each led the painter to dreaded shores. Even for great travelers, death is still the supreme journey.

The Storm (1823)

Turner discovered light during his trip to Italy in 1819. So thoroughly were light and poetry commingled in his work that they became indistinguishable. The watercolors he painted in Venice at the time are much more than an elegy to the city; they rain down light upon us. The extraordinary revelation that was to change Turner into the painter we find so captivating today, remains an enigma. There is nothing—no specific event, no sudden personal upheaval—to account for it. How did it come to pass that one day he simply "took it upon himself" to paint this way, to quote an apt turn of phrase used by Dr. Henri Danon-Boileau as the two of us sifted through the facts surrounding this question? Turner had an insatiable curiosity about the resources a painter has at his disposal. Did the sense of wonder inspired by the lagoon suddenly prompt him, in an uninhibited or even unconscious moment, to blend two blobs of color and immediately set about elaborating the possibilities which the mixture suggested to him?

Water and fire were the *primum mobile* of Turner's imagination. Could this union of water and sparkling light (a metaphor of fire) have been encouraged or triggered by technique alone? Watercolors, after all, draw their deepest secrets from water. For his part, Sir George Beaumont took exception to Turner's "endeavouring to make paintings in oil appear like watercolours, by which, in attempting to lightness and clearness, the force of oil painting is lost." So diverse and bewildering are the motives that determine the flow of an artist's emotions, the shudders of his intuition, the movement of his hands, that the unexpected can take on the aura of a miracle. The watercolors Turner painted in Venice were the dazzling aftermath of just such a miracle.

However, Turner was cautious when it came to oil paintings destined for collectors and institutions. Upon his return to London, he submitted *Rome from the Vatican* to the annual exhibition at the Royal Academy. However (ill. 58) complex this work may have been from a conceptual viewpoint, there was nothing innovative about it in terms of technique. The lovely light that caresses *The Bay of Baiae* turned somewhat harsh in *Mortlake Terrace,* while the (ill. 90, 77) sketches for the paintings commissioned by Lord Egremont (1828) fairly tremble with light, and the way it enlivens *George IV at the Provost's Banquet in the Parliament House, Edinburgh* (which, like the two works just men- (ill. 64) tioned, he kept secret) is nothing short of marvelous. A number of watercolors from the same period, sea pieces and studies of clouds in particular, were also transfigured by flashes of light.

We know that the uncanny painting entitled *Snow Storms: Hannibal and His Army Crossing the Alps* was inspired by a (ill. 51) thunderstorm which had worked Turner into a state of tremendous excitement. Walter Fawkes's son relates the incident as follows: "I proposed some better drawing block, but he said it did very well. He was absorbed—he was entranced...Presently the storm passed, and he finished. 'There,'said he, 'Hawkey; in two years you will see this again, and call it *Hannibal Crossing the Alps!'*" It strikes me that the key word here is "entranced": Turner's astounding ability to prolong a single moment of intense, jarring sensation through imagination and manual dexterity. *Calais Pier* likewise recounts an incident during which Turner very nearly lost his life as he (ill.31) approached the coast of France in 1802. The dramatic, daring treatment of the sea prompted his contemporaries to remark that his paintings were "rank, crude, and disordered" (Hoppner). The choice and order of those adjectives attest to the cruel oppression which the emotions and the senses were still subjected to in the name of good taste and the classical rules of representation. By contrast, how fresh and innovative Turner's approach seems for the time!

All of Turner's work is punctuated by sudden jolts of creativity that signal moments of upheaval in a "senseless" struggle with insuperable forces. The light he discovered in Venice shows up in the sketch for *Ulysses Deriding* (ill. 96) *Polyphemus—Homer's Odyssey* and reappears in the finished version ten years later. Through experiments the artist pursued in the last twenty years of his life, it progressed toward a dazzling, trancelike state of total integration. I should like to conceive of it as follows: collectively, these elements form a kind of constellation of lightning sensations—moments of bedazzlement, of fusion, of ecstacy—which reveal to us, however distant or obscured, Turner's desperate, sublimated search for a delight he never knew, a search which ended in disappointment. The physical and spiritual raptures of light spring from a common source that scorches and convulses whatever it touches. To quote Novalis: "Nothing more to stand in the way of love's voraciousness. The couple devours itself in mutual embraces; they feed on each other and need no other sustenance."

Water was a catalyst of supreme importance. I have already mentioned the role that the narcissism of nature played in Turner's imagination. Unquestionably all of the paintings that were never exhibited (1835-1845) partake of a moist, fluid domain drenched with light. This marriage, this interpenetration of light and water was powerful enough to trigger in these works a complete, indeed cosmic synthesis. This is what makes the light emanating from them so startling, so dazzling that we can no longer speak in terms of the antithesis of darkness. It rises to a higher plane, and for a blinding instant its glare does away with darkness altogether. Like all sudden ephemeral bursts of energy, it is at once violent and fragile. It is cannibalistic, it devours the universe, yet Turner's colors seem to brush ever so gently against the canvas as they throw back their image of the world. His water loses none of its transparency, nor do his skies. Amid this glowing phantasmagoria, where is the world? Where is reality? Erotic tension gives way to calm, just as water tends to subside and light to fade. Such is their proper fate: the tables are turned, and destruction, emptiness, darkness steal into view. In the recesses of his imagination, Turner discovered the ultimate solitude—death, or better still, love in death, love through death. Even if the artist stored away his ''backgrounds'' with the intention of adding human figures one day, they reveal even in their ''unfinished'' state the dynamic forces at work within his imagination. Satisfied or hesitant he would stop painting at a certain point in the belief that he could not develop them any further. There is no doubt in my mind that our unexpected discovery of the darkness lurking somewhere behind that screen of blinding light has a great deal to do with the emotional response its mystery elicits from us. There are few artists in the long history of painting who have managed to evoke mystery and eeriness through light instead of shadow.

The ultimate goal of painting has never been merely to copy the world. ''In no way does the tangible world—to which no art is ever beholden—enter into painting as the 'reality' we later think we see in it,'' writes André Malraux. ''This world is not an imitation of reality; it is the world of painting.''

From the moment it occurs, every relationship with a work of art activates a reality which differs from the world as we experience it in daily life. It brings into play not only that ''grey area'' of representation, but the forces of the imagination that are the true gauge of art. The ''reality'' of art is to be artistic. The much–admired fly on the grape and other virtuoso displays of *trompe l'oeil* boil down to a manual ability to copy something over again. Who would glorify such an obsession? No one but unfeeling rationalists, those laureated detractors of the imagination. Whether espoused as a theory or applied in schools of art, it is one and the same illusion (and delusion): regardless of how one goes about it, Baudelaire's ''queen of faculties,'' the imagination, remains an active participant in the creative process. In painting, the three–dimensional world must be readjusted for a two–dimensional canvas. The jug and fruit bowl in a Chardin or a Cézanne are not the same as those we see on the sideboard. Once they have been selected, transferred to a surface of a particular size, and painted within a predetermined system of colors and spatial relationships, they cease to be lowly objects. They become worthy of admiration and, in the end, acquire the power to evoke.

To reassure the timorous, or those in need of a handrail, there are always rules and theories. Ruskin, who in *Modern Painters* championed Turner's cause in the name of ''truth,'' wore himself out trying to convince them. His line of reasoning, for all its eloquence and zeal, comes as quite a disappointment to us today. It was predicated upon a set of historical preconceptions, endorsed by a class of art lovers who were alarmed by what the imagination had to reveal. Reasons have changed, forms have evolved, but the process remains the same. The breach is deep, irrevocable. Now again some gossamer threads are thrown from one side to the other, but the two worlds do not converge.

Nature remained the great model for Turner (as it did for Delacroix), but there is nothing in his notes or writings to indicate that he looked upon art as simply a carbon copy of nature. As he saw it, art was a self–contained system or process which could be defined only in its own terms. ''Eventually, no single touch of paint corresponded to any specific object,'' writes Laurence Gowing in his incisive commentary on Turner. ''The equivalence was between the whole configuration and the whole subject.''

Here was an idea too original—perhaps even too dangerous—to be publicly espoused. Indeed, it was much more common for his works to be greeted with obtuseness than with the admiration he so looked forward to. One of (ill. 108) the most imaginative and uncanny paintings Turner ever conceived, *The Slave Ship*, provoked an unfavorable reaction from William Makepeace Thackeray. Turns of phrase and imagery typical of contemporary evaluations of Turner ran riot in his review: ''...flakes of white laid on with a trowel; bladders of vermilion madly spirted here and there...; gasping dolphins redder than the reddest herrings; horrid spreading polypi, like huge, slimy, poached eggs...'' Back in 1816, Hazlitt, in one of his ''Round Table'' essays, had been only slightly kinder: ''[Turner's] pictures are however too much...representations not properly of the objects of nature as of the medium through which they were seen...The artist delights to go back to the first chaos of the world...Some one said of his landscapes that they were *pictures of nothing, and very like.*'' In another article Hazlitt dismissed ''the quackery of painting trees blue and yellow to produce the effect of green at a distance'' (Wilton). Not that Hazlitt's observations lack astuteness or insight, but what he railed against was precisely one of the idiosyncrasies that gave Turner's painting its daring novelty.

There is more to an artist's palette than technique; it is a choice that is rich in meaning. The arrangement of colors, their order, their distance from one another, the amount applied for each one—all of this reveals an artist's visual grid, how his hand moves and sees the world, his habits, his priorities. Favorite colors express his feelings, his imagination, his ''syntax.''

As he worked on *Ulysses Deriding Polyphemus,* an apprehensive Turner freed himself from academic restraints by (ill. 96) experimenting with a palette dominated by yellow, blue and red. These he referred to as "atmospheric colors," as opposed to "material colors." The artist's avowed determination to keep red and blue separate attests to his aversion to violet, which in his mind was the antithesis of yellow. Especially in his so-called unfinished paintings, he distributed warm and cool tones in a way that "evened out" the canvas chromatically, a way that softened and almost obliterated the contrasts of hue to be found in nature. He would wash them out with dazzling, devouring light. Chiaroscuro and classical shading gave way to pale, transparent, lustrous half-tones. His technique and way of looking at things were to be rediscovered by the exponents of *la peinture claire,* especially Monet and, to be sure, Bonnard in some of his later works. Starting with *Hannibal and His Army Crossing the Alps,* (ill. 51) Turner no longer considered black the opposite of light, but as a color in its own right, used for its own sake. Here is how Henri Matisse put it: "It was in this work *(Les Coloquintes*—1916) that I began to use pure black, not as a color of darkness, but as a color of light" (Alfred Barr).

Ulysses Deriding Polyphemus ushered in a new phase in Turner's career. The critic of the *Morning Herald* had good reason to feel ill at ease back in 1829: it was "coloring running mad—positive vermilion, positive indigo, and all the most glaring tints of green, yellow, and purple." But let us be careful not go to extremes. There was, it is true, more intuition than lucidity in Turner's approach. However, his empirical side transformed it into something which was better attuned to immediate concerns and needs. This fundamental chord, equal parts emotion and pragmatism, was to be sounded time and again throughout his career. In terms of intellectual virtousity, his *modus operandi* brings to mind the "Thirty-two Variations on an Original Theme in C Minor" which Beethoven composed in 1806. The initial theme provded the composer with a "pretext" for elaborating all possible combinations hidden within the original subject. With the same kind of deft, consummate craftsmanship, Turner tapped the potential hidden within the basic yellow-red-blue chord by varying shades from one work to the next in a continuous celebration of light. No more would sterile considerations of taste and propriety hamper his impulse to dare, even if it led to harshness and excess.

Yet, throughout his life Turner did make use of forms taught by the Academy; at least he realized that they could not simply be discarded. Having already gauged their value earlier in his career, he proceeded to adapt them to suit his own aims. Often his inventiveness was rooted in an outmoded tradition. Turner's oeuvre spans the entire first half of the nineteenth century, but he received his training in the eighteenth. For example, the startling modernity we see nowadays in those sketches of graduated bands of color might be a holdover from the classic technique of structuring the foreground, middle distance and far distance of a landscape into three zones of color: brown, green and blue, respectively.

Just the same, Turner was a self-taught painter. His unending quest for knowledge led him to ancient, Italian, and Dutch artists whose works were regarded at the time as exemplary. His conscientious and unscrupulous "borrowings" from his contemporaries have been duly enumerated and substantiated. However, it should be said in Turner's defense that the plagiarism he is accused of did not carry the pejorative overtones it does today. Now artistic property is protected by law, but artists then were not yet obliged to draw everything from within themselves and be indebted to no one. In those days, the heritage of art belonged to everyone. Beginning with the seventeenth century, this from of pastiche bore witness to an artist's culture and erudition; it was looked upon as a way of paying homage to the past. The more flagrant instances of deliberate "borrowing" among writers are especially celebrated cases in point. However, I cannot recall a single time in the long history of painting when an artist instituted proceedings in a court of law to claim credit for an "original" idea.

But even after this self-made man had established his niche within society, he hankered after the titles bestowed by recognized authorities. He had changed sides, this barber's son turned Academician, and still took naive pride in being able to show off what he knew. English to the core, he was just as self-satisfied when it came to his sense of humor (although the puns he reputedly delighted in were sometimes less than glorious). This still comes through in his painting: the little dog that was added to *Mortlake Terrace* was, and remains to this day, a kind of (ill. 77) "sight gag." The last-minute corrections he made prior to official varnishing days were often ironic retorts aimed at his colleagues, whether they meant him well or ill. Sometimes these adjustments were his way of parrying the impending blows of the aftermath—which, alas, all too often proved as aggressive as he feared. Some of his more peculiar or outlandish actions were triggered in this manner. In the melting pot of creation, there is room for every conceivable kind of mixture and combination, however unusual or far-fetched.

The eighteenth century witnessed a surge of interest in scientific theories. Science was beginning to break loose from subjective interpretations of natural phenomena. The new *zeitgeist* left its mark on Turner, who read the works of Newton and Moses Harris in search of verifications or fresh insights. He found himself once again intrigued by questions concerning vision and color perception, but he did not become familiar with Goethe's *Farbenlehre (Theory of Colors)*—published in 1810 and translated by his friend Charles Eastlake—until 1840. He (ill. 133) wasted little time in mentioning that celebrated name in title, but since his demonstration of Goethe's theory is anything but obvious, perhaps he did so to keep in step with current trends. In any event, Goethe's ideas did not reach him until late in his career and had little, if any effect on the system he had already worked out. Like

Goethe, Turner had chosen yellow as the color nearest to light; he too had "perceived a rising intensification of yellow and blue towards red." The notes he jotted down in the margin of his copy of *Theory of Colors* lead one to believe that, in certain matters, Turner even deemed himself more advanced than Goethe. I dare say, Turner's imagination was such that he thought directly in colors.

Quite naturally, art historians, armed with their in–depth knowledge of Turner's work, have readily credited him with sowing the seeds of Impressionism. However, this alleged affiliation needs to be cast in a very special light. First of all, one must take into account the diversity of the individuals which made up this movement. Only Monet was an Impressionist. All of the other painters followed the course he charted for a while, then went their own way.

Second, at the time of Monet's stint in London—both Pissarro and he had fled their homeland in the wake of the Franco–Prussian War—most of the Turners on display at the National Gallery were from the painter's "classical" phase, when he was trying to emulate Claude Lorrain. The paintings that really played with fire, technically speaking, were locked away in the museum's storerooms and could not be seen. Thus, Monet and Pissarro were denied access to the very works that everyone today points to as the harbingers of *la peinture claire*. In the final analysis, apathy on the part of institutions like the National Gallery was partly to blame for the long period of uncertainty the Impressionists went through and the public's belated recognition of their work. The younger generation's taste and demand for the absolute did the rest.

Thomas Fearnley: Turner on Varnishing Day (1835)

Pissarro recalled the lessons he had learned during his stay in London in a letter to W. Dewhurst (November, 1902): "We also visited the museums," he wrote. "The watercolors and paintings of Turner and Constable, as well as the paintings of Old Crome certainly influenced us." But he revealed himself more fully to his son, Lucien, in a letter dated May 8, 1903. "Turner and Constable," he wrote, "though helpful, confirmed our suspicion that they had not understood analysis of shadows, which is a weak spot in Turner's works, something he did for effect. As for division of color, Turner convinced us, if not of its accuracy, then of its value as a technique." However, in a letter from a number of Impressionists—Pissarro, Monet, Renoir, Sisley, among others—to Sir Coutts Lindsay in 1885, they state that "their aim is to restore to art scrupulously accurate observation of nature by making every effort to render moving forms as well as the fleeting effects of light. They cannot forget that they were preceded in this endeavor by the great master of the English school, the illustrious Turner." Of course, I am perfectly aware that this collective letter in which Monet defers to Turner was addressed to an Englishman; it smacks of diplomacy. No doubt Monet actually felt that the "classical" Turners he saw in London's National Gallery simply confirmed the legitimacy of his own experiments.

However, as time passed and other works came to light, the Impressionists discovered in Turner a painter whose approach could indeed open up uncharted horizons. Be that as it may, Monet was to continue along quite a different path. Monet, standard–bearer of the school, the only member of the group to follow the philosophy and original spirit of Impressionism to its logical conclusion in the fabulous *Nymphéas* (Musée de l'Orangerie, Paris), did not get what he looked for out of Turner's work. Since Impressionism's aim was "the scrupulously accurate observation of nature," Monet had a clear conscience: their aim was different.

Raymond Koechlin alludes to this in an article in *Art et Décoration* a year after Monet's death (1927). "It had often been said that Turner had a great deal to do with Monet's development," he writes. "He [Monet] always denied it and, in fact, it had begun long before he became familiar with Turner's work in the National Gallery. Moreover, he admitted privately that he, Monet, had an aversion to him because of the romantic exuberance of his imagination." A letter Claude Debussy wrote to Jacques Durand in March, 1908, sums up the ambiguity of the Turner–Monet relationship. "The *Images* shall not be completely finished when you get back, but I hope to play a substantial part of it for you…I am trying to do something 'different'—bits of 'reality,' if you will—what imbeciles refer to as 'Impressionism.' No label has been more inappropriately used, especially by art critics, who do not hesitate to attach it to Turner, the finest creator of mystery that Art has ever known" (François Lesure). The portrait which *la peinture claire* drew of reality was strange indeed: "divided" colors, shadows rendered in colors complementary to the colors of objects, black excluded because it does not occur in nature. From the very first Impressionist exhibition in 1874, the thing that stood out in everyone's mind was its "imprecision." It was an unfamiliar kind of painting, out–of–focus, devoid of well-defined contours. This often repeated objection was partly responsible for the Cubist reaction and the triumphant return of form. But even that did not silence the voices of reproach, and we hear them to this day.

There was more at stake in this clash between fluidity and definition than aesthetics; it involved a different way of feeling, another way of looking at the world. Painting is inconceivable without form of one kind or another. Jackson Pollock delineated forms as he splashed colors across his canvas. The great abstract painters were impeccable draftsmen. There is not a single painting worthy of admiration which does not display a superb handling of line. But light tends to dissolve outlines. How, then, could they be made visible even when subjected to the evaporative stresses of light? This was the dilemma that faced Turner and the Impressionists alike.

Turner and Monet arrived at a similar solution (allowing for the idiosyncrasies of the former's distinctive style).

For both of them, paint itself is what creates form. The dynamics of the brush—spatters, streaks, flourishes, splashes, slashes—bring form into being. To compensate for blurred outlines, pigments turn into contours and, in so doing, coalesce into recognizable forms with the help of the viewer's memory. A "hidden" composition of swirling triangles emerges from the clustered strokes which sweep across *Snow Storm*, bewildering though the brushwork may be. Awash in a silvery mist, the spots of paint that make up *George IV at the Provost's Banquet in the Parliament House, Edinburgh* do not bring objects into sharp focus, but we can make out the rough equivalents of chandeliers, soldiers and chamberlains nonetheless. Those spots delineate form. (ill. 143) (ill.64)

To give an example from Monet's oeuvre, consider the famous *Cathedral* series of 1891-1894: shattered surfaces teeming with controlled strokes of varying thickness. There is more to form than outlines. There is not a single well-defined shape in the marvelous charcoal sketches of Seurat. Turner, for his part, came to terms with this problem through his handling of impasto. Now, one would think that light (what could be less tangible?) would have to be rendered with the lightest brushwork imaginable, and this is how painters, including Monet, generally went about it. Supreme lightness of touch is the hallmark of the shimmering scenes Monet painted at Argenteuil. With Turner, however, the process is reversed: light bursts forth from thick brushwork. At the same time, applying a light color over darker layers was still a way of remaining loyal to the classical mode of attack, by which a painter guides our eyes from the lightest to the darkest tones. Jean Clay has correctly summed up the "Turner paradox" as follows: "Extreme diffuseness and intagibility are rendered by extreme harshness and heaviness."

Turner's wonderfully subtle eye was as refined as a musician's ear. The latter can pick out the murmur of a single instrument as an orchestra plays, and its timbre tinges the overall effect in a unique and vital way. For example, in the upper right corner of *Norham Castle*, Turner very gently scraped the glossy surface of paint with the handle of his brush. Invisible in reproductions, these scratchings add a quivering effect to the white, moiréd surface in this area of the composition.

That is but one surprise the fleeting effects of natural light hold in store for the onlooker. It dances about the rough edges of paint and glances off the edges of scrapings. This property was well known to all "expressive" painters: Magnasco, Hals, Rembrandt, Delacroix, Goya, and more recently, Braque, Nicolas de Staël, and Lanskoy. With certain artists it ossified into an endlessly repeated effect and, in such cases, deserves the pejorative label of "device." In Turner's work, however, it expresses a state of visual exasperation, an unpredictable, and therefore mysterious aspect of his bewildering imagination. As Nicolas de Staël put it: "There are a thousand vibrations to be absorbed for every one of [Turner's] strokes."

When paint is feverishly applied over the surface of the canvas, it is bound to leave smudges and mishaps in its wake. Turner's experience with Leonardo, Alexander Cozens, and George Romney made him aware of the evocative, enigmatic subjects which could emerge from haphazard blobs of paint. As he worked, his imagination—whether alert to outside stimuli or left to its own devices—seems to have responded to the vagaries of his brush as it collided with pigment. Images which people incorrectly ascribe to chance would take shape before his eyes. If in some mold forming on a rock he perceived a building, a battle, a face, or a fish, it was because his imagination induced him to identify them as such. For a painter, the shapeless is always straining to assume a shape; in his eyes, it always has a shape. In this respect, the romantic originality of Turner also lies in his receptiveness. Images and ideas leaped out at him as his hand applied pressure to the moving brush, and he immediately seized upon them. Thus, a stray mark left by his tools could take on an identity. The carnivorous fish in *The Slave Ship*, driven wild by the smell of blood around the slave's leg, emerged from a tremor in the paint and (ill.108) triggered a suitable hallucination to make the horror of the carnage that much more immediate and intense. The fantastic beast skimming through the frothy sea in *Sunrise with Sea Monster* bore down upon the painter the moment his laboring brushes created it: it seems to spring as much from the restless pigments as from his sense of terror. Later on, this same kind of susceptibility or impressionability was to reappear in the work of Paul Klee. The adjectives "unusual" and "unexpected" are rigid concepts; they alone cannot account for this receptivity, which is of a different order and occurs only in the uncertain, unfathomable world of the artist. The images generated by a painter's openness to suggestion awaken within us echoes we ourselves are unaware of, echoes which only our emotions are capable of liberating and identifying.

The tools a painter uses often influence and determine how his hands move and the kinds of marks which will be left embedded in the greasy paint. Early in his career, a trusting Turner opened his studio to everyone. Then he must have realized that the visits his would-be friends were paying him smacked of espionage. After each of his meetings with the painter, Farington wasted no time writing down what he saw. Although the historical importance of this information is undeniable, the fact remains that his dry observations read like recipes for insipid stews. Some noticed odd rituals out of the corner of their eye when they were at Turner's studio. He would ill-treat his fragile, limpid watercolors, among other works, in the fervor of creation. He would immerse them in water, tear the paper with his nails, squash paint with his thumb, spit on pigments.

Unfortunately, it never occurred to anyone to leave a detailed account of how Turner ground his colors, how he took on his palette the number of colors he deemed necessary, how he added water to the solid cakes of gouache or watercolor and then rubbed the mixture down to the desired consistency. Knowing this might have opened up marvelous paths leading to the hidden domain of his imagination. In an incisive passage on this subject, Gaston Bachelard notes: ''This reverie which springs from the working of colors necessarily goes hand in hand with a special desire for power, the masculine delight in penetrating a substance, feeling the inside of a substance, probing textures, vanquishing the earth as intimately as water does, recapturing an elemental vigor, taking part in the struggle between elements, sharing in a force whose power to dissolve is merciless.''

Afterwards his studio became a ''shrine'' which only his housekeeper-assistant had the privilege to enter. Shortly after the artist's death, Reverand Trimmer's son was finally able to visit the studio. ''In the center of the [circular] table was a raised box with a circle in the center with side compartments; a good contrivance for an artist, though I had never seen one of the kind before…In the centre were his colours…cobalt there was to be sure, but also several bottles of ultramarine of various depths, and smalts of various intensities. There was also some verditer,…a large bottle of blanc d'argent and another of lake white…a large bottle of chrome. There were also a bottle of tincture of rhubarb and some iodine, but whether for artistical or medicinal use I cannot say…The palette—at least that in use, for he possessed two large splendid ones—was a homely piece of square wood, with a hole for the thumb. Grinding colours on a slab was not his practice, his dry colors were rubbed on the palette with cold-drawn oil. His colours were mixed daily, and he was very particular…His brushes were of the humblest description, mostly round hog's tools…I was informed by his housekeeper that he used the long brush exclusively for the rigging of ships,…and formerly he showed my father some Chinese brushes he was in he habit of using. Mrs. Danby told me that when he had nearly finished a picture, he took it to the end of a long gallery, and put on the last touches…There were cakes of water-colour fastened on a leaf, the centres of which were worn away, the commonest colours, one a cake of verditer, one or two sable brushes and lead pencils, not in wood…He seems to have purchased detail-views of foreign scenery, of which there was a large assortment well thumbed; the drudgery of the art, of which masterminds avail themselves…There was also a bureau of old colours and oils,…a bottle of spirit-varnish and a preparation of tar,…old bladders of raw umber and other dark earths…The above, with numerous unframed pictures around the apartment, were the contents of his painting-room, which had no skylight. It had been originally the drawing-room and had a good north light, with two windows.''

Nothing uncanny: just simple, lowly tools. The pictures he carried into a ''long gallery'' invalidate the assertion that his audacious style was actually the result of an eye disorder. There is nothing in Trimmer's account to satisfy our burning curiosity, no startling revelation to unlock a mystery that clearly remains unsolved. As the visitor rightly concludes, ''I must confess that a deep melancholy pervaded me as I made this inspection. Till of late years, I had been in the habit of entering the house from my childhood; the owner was no more; he stood alone in the world, and his race was extinct.''

I. FORMATIVE YEARS

Self-portrait (1790)

If somewhere in History the trail of humanity's progress is to be found, it is on the path leading to freedom and light.

Johann Paul Friedrich Richter

One of the two self-portraits we have of Turner is a painting from 1798, when the artist was twenty–three. The (page 2) sober, pensive face looming out of a dark background blends in with a rather casual opening in his jacket. The eyes are two matching ovals of unequal size. The necktie knotted beneath his high collar is framed by a light–colored triangle of waistcoat lining. The lighting, already skilfully distributed, carefully models the volumes and planes which make up his face and brings out the highlights of his apparel. The unctuous, but understated brushwork is in keeping with the general severity of the portrait. This young man shows neither complacency nor commiseration as he observes himself. He is serious, tense, above all enigmatic. The limited palette of light ochers and subdued reddish accents further adds to the overall impression. A comparison with the portraits of young, elegant, aristocratic idlers living at the time makes the character of this stubborn, dour young man all the easier to read. There is nothing here of the young wolf ravenous for new sensations. His aspirations were of a different order and called for concentration and tenacity.

The other self-portrait is a sketch drawn in 1790, when Turner was only fifteen: shoulder–length hair, locks spread across his forehead, large, inquisitive eyes. The striped waistcoast has seen much wear: it is creased with use, and the button slips all too easily through the buttonhole. The color is brisk and dashing, while the modeling already bespeaks his sensitivity to light and shadow. Here is a lad of humble birth, fresh, alert, whose imperceptible smile tells us that he is no doubt very inquisitive, no doubt scoffing.

We have very little information about young Turner's formal education and apprenticeship. Probably he attended schools in the villages or towns he spent time in, since Walter Thornbury, his first (and, as is generally acknowledged, highly dubious) biographer, mentions that ''old schoolfellows of Turner's used to say that his first attempts at art had been drawings of birds and flowers and trees from the schoolroom windows.'' Throughout this period, Turner did not encounter a single painter of repute who might have taken him under his wing. Like many other apprentices, he started out by copying and coloring. His work showed enough talent to bring in two pence a plate. Only death could part him from an engraving of Oxford he had done when he was twelve.

At the age of fourteen, Turner already felt encouraged enough to stand on his own two feet. His attentive father—he also knew how to make the most of an opportunity—hung up his son's drawings in his shop and sold them to customers at prices ranging from two to three shillings. His earliest book of sketches and studies from nature (Oxford and vicinity) dates from 1789. Young Turner's aptitude for art was indisputable and acknowledged; his mind was made up. Thus, his family had no recourse but to further his education. ''My son, Sir, is going to be a painter,'' his father, the shopkeepr, would proudly proclaim (Thornbury).

Turner made his first contacts with the official art world at the Royal Academy Schools in 1789. He studied with Thomas Malton, who specialized in architectural subjects. It is likely that there were also a few sessions in the studio of the architect Hardwick. This particular branch of the fine arts satisfied the public's curiosity and thus provided opportunities for guaranteed profit and security—an advantage in the eyes of any family worried about the uncertainties of ''artistic'' ventures. Turner could look forward to a comfortable career that would enable him to earn a living without sinking into the much–dreaded licentiousness of bohemianism.

The training he received usually consisted of drawing plaster casts after ancient works, or nude models, but he also indulged now and again in an exercise after nature to satisfy his own curiosity. After a year he judged himself ready and decided to show his work. True, there was nothing particularly daring about *The Archbishop's Palace,* (ill.4) *Lambeth,* the watercolor he submitted to the Academy in 1790. Probably it was based on a sketch he had made earlier on in the so–called Oxford sketchbook. But it did attract the attention of the critics.

In 1791–92, during another tour of the English countryside, he stayed at the home of a friend of his father's, a furrier and gluemaker by the name of John Narraway. There he discovered the marvelous gorges of the Avon and (ill. 16) "the picturesque beauties of the South Welsh coast, the mountains of the border country, and the Wye valley, which he could easily reach from Bristol" (Andrew Wilton). The motives and aims of this trip were much the same as those of the painter's other excursions; thus the stint at the Narraways offords us a priceless glimpse into his daily life.

Turner was a restless traveler who made his numerous tours with very specific goals in mind: to jot down sketches and notes and, abetted by his prodigious visual memory, to build up a store of information for future reference. Sketching from life was a lifetime occupation for Turner. He made notes about the form, elevation, plan and articulation of architectural subjects, about color, about lighting—all of which he would rework once he returned to his studio. There, unhampered by the discomforts of working in the open, he could perform his feverish, painstaking ritual of creation at his leisure. The reaction of his hosts during this particular stay in the country reveals that they considered the young artist unsociable and interested above all in his drawings, that he would set out at dawn and now and again forget mealtimes, much to the consternation of the mistress of the house. In short, they regarded Turner as the very antithesis of a well-bred young man: casual in his behavior, a careless dresser, ill-mannered, uncommunicative. Nevertheless, the Narraways appreciated the drawings that Turner gave them and were quite happy to sell them when the opportunity presented itself. Even if we ignore that last stroke, we can see which way the wind was blowing!

Just the same, his whole life long Turner was taken to task for his uncouth cockney accent, shabby–looking appearance, carelessness, undignified bearing, and inability to make a good impression on visitors. The opinion which Delacroix expressed in 1855 was much the same: Thomas Armstrong "spoke to me of Turner, who bequeathed a hundred thousand pounds for a charitable institution for poor and disabled artists. He lived like a miser with an old housekeeper. I recall receiving him only once; I was residing on Quai Voltaire at the time (1833). He did not make much of an impression upon me. He looked like an English farmer, with his black, coarse–looking attire, rugged shoes, and dour, unresponsive expression." But just as nothing is of a piece, so—inexplicable tendency of the human heart!—people never elicit the same reactions. Thus, it is only right that the remarks of Clara Wheeler be added here. (Clara's father, the watercolorist William Frederick Wells, was, in Turner's own words, "the best friend I ever had in my life.") "Of all the light-hearted, merry creatures I ever knew, Turner was the most so; and the laughter and fun that abounded when he was an inmate of our cottage was inconceivable, particularly with the juvenile members of the family...He was a firm, affectionate friend to the end of his life, his feelings were seldom seen on the surface, but they were deep and enduring. No one would have imagined, under that rather rough and cold exterior how very strong were the affections which lay hidden beneath."

It was around this time that, in the best tradition of friendly exploitation, Dr. Thomas Monro, a well–known collector, hired (among others) Turner and Thomas Girtin, a superbly gifted watercolorist, to make watercolors from drawings left unfinished by the great John Robert Cozens. According to Finberg, each participant in this curious venture saw to a particular phase of the operation: Girtin completed the drawings and Turner applied the washes. This well–intentioned hoax—more widespread than is generally believed—enabled the young artists to make ends meet for some three years. But the real advantage was that it brought them in close touch with the work of one of the country's preeminent watercolorists.

In a book entitled *English Painting,* Jean–Jacques Mayoux comments further on this reflective activity of Turner's early years—"reflective" implying both contemplation and images thrown back by a mirror (1).

Dr. Monro:
Turner (c. 1796)

Having acquired what he considered sufficient mastery of his craft, Turner decided to exhibit regularly at the Royal Academy without waiting to complete his formal education. This august institution was founded in 1768 under the auspices of George III, and Sir Joshua Reynolds served as its president until 1792. An earnest theoretician, Reynolds took it upon himself to codify in his writings the tyrannical rules of art and to provide in his work a model for their implementation. The hierarchy of genres he defined and laid down for painters matched point for point that which had been prescribed and applied throughout Europe ever since the seventeenth century. (For one thing, landscape did not enjoy a prominent position, unless the subject was historical.)

During this period and for many years thereafter, every artistic career hinged upon the opinions expressed by the members of the Royal Academy. There was no way of making oneself known to art enthusiasts except by taking part in the annual exhibitions mounted by this distinguished institution. To have one's work included in a Royal Academy show was a token of success. Showered with royal honors, affiliated with the upper classes, this highly esteemed group of painters dispensed commissions, forged artistic reputations, and bestowed glory upon those it favored. Even in England, landscape painting was not the best way to reap these rewards, although the passion for topographical scenes in the latter part of the eighteenth century did provide artists with some chance of getting their work into the public eye. In an illuminating letter to the Earl of Hardwick, Gainsborough declined a request to paint a site which had been specified to him.

Anyone wishing to succeed at even the "inferior" (but lucrative) genre of landscape painting still had to run the Academy gauntlet. And so Turner had to bide his time. His patience and steadfastness of purpose were rewarded with some strokes of good luck. In 1793 he was awarded a prize by the Society of Arts; in 1794 the first engraving taken from one of his sketches was published, and his contribution to the Royal Academy exhibition that year brought him critical attention. In 1795 he entered into relations with Sir Richard Colt Hoare, a wealthy notable who became his first patron; he also received commissions from Lord Viscount Malden, Fifth Earl of Essex, and Edward Lascelles, First Earl of Harewood. All three of these distinguished gentlemen requested Turner to make topographical drawings and watercolors that depicted specific places or panoramic views. Though Gainsborough commented upon the accuracy of such views in a letter to the Earl of Hardwick, the real challenge facing an artist was to shift things about in a way that gave the landscapes a "picturesque" quality.

In his essay entitled *The Theory of Painting*, the philosopher Jonathan Richardson described the picturesque as that which enobles and uplifts the human spirit. This theory was further developed during the eighteenth century, and by the time of Sir Uvedale Price, the term "picturesque" had taken on a meaning that considerably broadened people's interest in nature. "In general, I believe, it [the word picturesque] is applied to every object, and every kind of scenery, which has been or might be represented with good effect in painting—just as the word beautiful, when we speak of visible nature, is applied to every object and every kind of scenery that in any way gives pleasure to the eye—and these seem to be the significations of both words, taken in their most extended and popular sense." (*Essay on the Picturesque*, 1794–98).

The longer the debate dragged on, the more the word took on different shades of meaning. However, these sundry concepts of the picturesque remained so fresh and urgent, if somewhat confused, in people's minds that, in order to get his point across, Ruskin felt it necessary to bring it up once again in a chapter of *Modern Painters*. He attempts to make a distinction between the "inferior" picturesque of Stanfield (*Coast Scenery*) and, as one would suspect, the "superior" picturesque of Turner (*L'Ecluse, Liber Studiorum*) based upon the degree of "sympathy" of the artist. Sympathy: another nineteenth–century catchword that provided philosophers with ample opportunity for intellectual wrangling. Ruskin's idea of sympathy incorporated an association with all of nature that was total; a humility that permitted a search for beauty and grace in even the simplest subject. It was an idea that had endured since ancient times, and Shaftesbury, whose thinking influenced artistic theories in the eighteenth century, reaffirmed it when he stated that beauty and goodness were one and the same, and that such impressions spring from the spirit rather than the mind.

Ruins of Kirkstall Abbey

Thus, every work executed by an artist (in this case, a painter) was supposed to uplift people's souls and direct them toward the Good. The picturesque was regarded as one way of achieving this goal. Skillful arrangement of components was supposed to provide the viewer's soul with the chance to be exalted, while his mind would be improved and guided along the right path. From this exaltation of the soul—which was considered a higher plane in its own right—there emerged yet another aesthetic distinction and category known as the "sublime." Only great artists could reach this transcendent level that was the hallmark of "High Art." It was an exemplary quality that turned the artist who possessed it into an exceptional being. Yet, whatever the virtues of an artist or his subject may have been, this lofty goal could not be achieved by way of topographical views. In the minds of philosophers, artists, and art lovers alike, they belonged to a genre of minor importance. People collected them; the upper and middle classes decorated their homes with them; the wealthy commissioned them, but their limitations were known and accepted. Perhaps it was those very limitations that account for the enormous success of topographical art at the time.

Turner drew and colored *The Pantheon the Morning after the Fire* on two different occasions and ended up with two (ill. 6) very different versions. One of the watercolors is a hectic genre scene, its action attractively depicted; in the other, the charred walls as Turner observed them after the disaster create a sense of drama. Here the artist's penchant for theatricality quickly came to the fore. We are taken beyond a straightforward description of an event and into the realm of tragedy; we can feel the crushing presence of fate. Throughout his career, Turner was to oscillate between these two poles, these two aesthetic extremes that were defined by Edmund Burke and William Gilpin. Choice of subject was of paramount importance. No "great" work of art could be undertaken without a "design," and all of the elements an artist arranged within a composition were supposed to divulge his "design" and allow the viewer to interpret it.

Turner's decision to paint the great monuments of Gothic art, the national art of England, was part shrewdness, part concession to tradition. The public of late eighteenth–century England felt a particularly keen need to renew its ties with its past. It was not difficult for art enthusiasts to attach metaphorical interpretations to these once awesome works of architecture, now ravaged by the centuries, eroded by the elements, and overgrown with vegetation. Ruins gratified their sense of melancholy and the vague yearnings of their emotions. A lone tree in an immense landscape evoked man's solitude in the face of creation and the seasons, or it could be a way of speaking out against tyranny, thus an ode to freedom. The monuments of the past not only brought history to life, but recalled the triumph of mind over matter, symbolized man's determination, glorified the powers of his intellect and, by contrast, pointed out the failings of his passions. Although the general public was not indifferent to the formal qualities of a work of art, its mode of perception, and chief delight, was decidedly literary. The purpose of art was to inspire noble thoughts. In this respect, Elie Faure is justified in reproaching English painters for their "literariness." The time had not yet come for painting to be appreciated in and of itself. It would come with Constable.

Especially interesting in terms of lighting and use of a foreground arch to direct the viewer's eyes is Turner's (ill. 8, 3) series of superb watercolors of English cathedrals (*St. Anselm's Chapel, Canterbury, Tintern Abbey, Llanthony Abbey*). The resulting contrasts emphasize and dramatize the impression of receding space. The space is soothed or disturbed, as the case may be, by shafts of light that were doubtless more imagined than real. Some of the effects in these watercolors appear to have been borrowed from Piranesi, whose series of *Carceri d'invenzione* engravings was circulating in England at the time. In addition, Turner's ability to hold back, then speed up our pace of observation brings to mind some of Guardi's scenes of Venice.

The foreground in all of the ''cathedral'' watercolors is dark and carefully positioned in a way that securely anchors the composition and counterbalances the lighting in the other areas of the picture. But the foreground could also come alive with bright, shimmering reflections (*Warwick Castle and Bridge* and both versions of *Magdalen Tower and Bridge, Oxford*) or provide the artist with a chance to display his consummate treatment of shifting, overlapping images reflected in water (*Old Bridge, Shrewsbury*). At issue still was where Turner placed figures—workers, shepherds, tourists—to give a sense of the monument's scale. Although he rendered them in minute detail, they would always be a source of concern and difficulty; he did all he could to conceal as adroitly as possible his lack of real interest in the human figure.

In these early works, feeling and technique overlapped, but never intermingled. True, Turner had no difficulty varying his subjects as he oscillated between his emotions and his anxiousness to please. But he felt cramped and was trying to find ways of circumventing the limitations of the genre. The denseness and decisiveness of his watercolors were more typical of oil painting, which he began to explore at this time. As the century drew to a close, Turner and Thomas Girtin were regarded as two of the finest watercolorists alive.

The distinction that philosophers made between the paths leading to the picturesque and those leading to the sublime more than accounts for Turner's desire to familiarize himself with what was for him a new technique. Mastering oil painting would allow him to become an artist of rank and win the flattering esteem of his fellow-countrymen. His sense of urgent industriousness, his thirst for knowledge, his unflagging tenacity—everything about Turner showed that he was driven by ambition, and for good reason: who would not be tempted by a future of greatness? And how could someone who was twenty—and English besides—fail to heed the irresistible call of the high seas?

St. Anselm's Chapel,
Canterbury (R.A. 1794)

1. CATHEDRAL CHURCH AT LINCOLN
R.A. 1795 — Watercolor over pencil, 45 x 35 cm
British Museum, London.

2. RADLEY HALL FROM THE SOUTH-EAST
1789 — Pencil and watercolor, 29.4 x 43.5 cm
British Museum, London.

3. LLANTHONY ABBEY
1794 — Pencil and watercolor, 32.7 x 42.2 cm
British Museum, London.

4. THE ARCHBISHOP'S PALACE, LAMBETH
R.A. 1790 — Pencil and watercolor, 26.3 x 37.8 cm
Indianapolis Museum of Art.

5. NEWPORT CASTLE
c. 1796 — Watercolor, 23 x 30.2 cm
British Museum, London.

6. THE PANTHEON, THE MORNING AFTER THE FIRE
R.A. 1792 — Watercolor over pencil, 39.5 x 51.1 cm
British Museum, London.

7. TOM TOWER, CHRIST CHURCH, OXFORD
c. 1793 — Pencil and watercolor, 31.5 x 24 cm
British Museum, London.

8. THE INTERIOR OF THE RUINS OF TINTERN ABBEY
c. 1794 — Watercolor, 36 x 25.5 cm
British Museum, London.

9. LANDAFF CATHEDRAL, SOUTH WALES
R.A. 1796 — Pencil and watercolor, 35.7 x 25.8 cm
British Museum, London.

9.

10. ST. ERASMUS IN BISHOP ISLIP'S CHAPEL
R.A. 1796 — Pencil and watercolor, 54.6 x 39.8 cm
British Museum, London

11. LINCOLN CATHEDRAL
c. 1794 — Pencil, 26 x 20 cm
British Museum, London.

12. KIRKSTALL ABBEY, YORKSHIRE
1797 — Pencil
British Museum, London.

13. CONWAY CASTLE
c. 1798 — Pencil, 32 x 47 cm
British Museum, London.

14. KIRKSTALL ABBEY, YORKSHIRE
1797 — Watercolor, 51.4 x 74.9 cm
Fitzwilliam Museum, Cambridge.

15. THE WESTERN TOWER, ELY CATHEDRAL
1794 — Watercolor over pencil, 21 x 28 cm
British Museum, London

16. VIEW ON THE RIVER AVON NEAR WALLIS'S WALL,
    BRISTOL
    1791 — Watercolor, 24 x 29.5 cm
    British Museum, London.

17. THE CASCADES, HAMPTON COURT, HEREFORDSHIRE
    1795 — Pencil and watercolor, with some gouache, 31.4 x 41.1 cm
    Victoria and Albert Museum, London.

II. LAUNCHING A CAREER—THE SUBLIME

> "The truly beautiful lies in what makes man better."
> *Madame de Staël*

"'This,' said Turner, with emotion, taking up a particular engraving, 'made me a painter.' It was a green mezzo-tinto, a Vandervelde—an upright; a single large vessel running before the wind and bearing up bravely against the waves" (Thornbury). Perhaps it was an irrepressible longing for the mother denied him in childhood that brought him back time and again to the rocking motion of the sea…

In point of fact, the "green mezzotinto" in question was probably a work by Elisha Kirkall that had been widely circulated in London during the eighteenth century. Whether it was a purely emotional reaction to the encounter or a symbiosis on a deeper level of the painter's unconscious, we cannot say. The fact remains, however, that the first oils Turner officially exhibited at the Royal Academy were seascapes in which the dominant color was green. Indeed, "sea pieces" of this kind were to be a recurrent subject during the next five years of his career. There is an eerie, glaucous cast to the light of *Fishermen at Sea (The Cholmeley Sea Piece),* which is generally acknowledged to be the first canvas Turner sent to an Academy exhibition (1796). The critic John Williams (who went by the pseudonym of Anthony Pasquin) wrote, "We recommend the piece, which hangs in the Ante-Room, to the consideration of the judicious." Surrounded by a diamond–shaped area of moonlit billows, two small craft filled with fishermen are struggling with the elements. The dramatic *chiaroscuro* and the muted light dancing on the surface of the sea bring to mind the lighting effects of Rembrandt, even more the unsettling night pieces of Joseph Wright of Derby. In *Fishermen at Sea,* Turner sounded what was to become one of the great leitmotifs of his oeuvre, man's battle with hostile forces, and in the process demonstrated how skillfully he could exploit the pictorial conventions of the day. He was playing the trump card of the sublime to advantage.

Fishermen at Sea ("The Cholmeley Sea Piece")

In *A Philosophical Inquiry into the Origin of our Ideas of the Sublime and the Beautiful*, Edmund Burke singles out darkness as one of the characteristics that make the sublime such a gripping experience. "To make any thing very terrible," he observes, "obscurity seems in general to be necessary. When we know the full extent of any danger, when we can accustom our eyes to it, a great deal of apprehension vanishes." He submits as proof the description of Death in Book II of Milton's *Paradise Lost*. "In this description all is dark, uncertain, confused, terrible, and sublime to the last degree."

But the supreme attribute of the sublime, Burke argues, is its power to trigger the imagination. "The mind is hurried out of itself by a crowd of great and confused images; which affect because they are crowded and confused."…"Another source of the sublime is *infinity*," we read later on. "Infinity has a tendency to fill the mind with that sort of delightful horror, which is the most genuine effect and truest test of the sublime." This summoning forth of intense emotion in the latter part of the eighteenth century—only the beginning, we now realize, of a headlong plunge into nature—was part and parcel of that "elevated style" which Burke claimed was more easily achieved in poetry than in painting. "Painting, when we have allowed for the pleasure of imitation, can only affect simply by the images it presents." This, then, was one of the sources of romanticism, to the extent that the term connotes an impulsive spilling over of emotion. "To me high mountains are a feeling," claimed Byron when he discovered Switzerland in 1816. A new image of the world was in the making, an image steeped in "feeling" and an outpouring of emotion. Burke had taken a stand against the old concept of the imagination that Pascal had set forth in the *Pensées*: "It is man's dominant faculty, the mistress of error and falsehood, and all the more deceitful because it does not always deceive; for it would be an infallable rule of truth if it were the infallible rule of falsehood. But being for the most part false, it gives no indication of its real quality because it puts the same stamp on true and false alike. I am not speaking of madmen; I am speaking of the wisest of men, and it is among them that imagination has the greatest power of conviction. Reason protests, to no avail; it cannot decide the value of things."

Brightelmstone (c. 1796)

The following is an excerpt from the thirteenth discourse (December 11, 1786) that Sir Joshua Reynolds delivered as president of the Royal Academy: ''To illustrate this principle by comparison with other arts, I shall now produce some instances to show that they, as well as our own art, renounce the narrow idea of nature…and apply to that reason only which informs us not what imitation is—a natural representation of a given object—but what is natural for the imagination to be delighted with.'' There follows a comparison of the resources used by poetry and painting. It is, Reynolds argues, through the ''licence it assumes of deviating from actual nature'' and its use of ''a language in the highest degree artificial, a construction of measured words such as never is, nor ever was used by man,'' that poetry shows itself to be ''full as capable of affording such gratification.''

At last Reynolds comes to the point and brings in the question of style by way of Nicolas Poussin and Claude Lorrain. ''If we suppose a view of nature represented with all the truth of the *camera obscura,* and the same scene represented by a great artist, how little and mean will the one appear in comparison of the other, where no superiority is supposed from the choice of subject. The scene shall be the same, the difference only will be in the manner in which it is presented to the eye.''

''Like the history–painter,'' he continues, ''a painter of landscapes in this style and with this conduct sends the imagination back into antiquity; and, like the poet, he makes the elements sympathize with his subject: whether the clouds roll in volumes, like those of Titian or Salvator Rosa, or, like those of Claude, are gilded with the setting sun; whether the mountains have sudden and bold projections, or are gently sloped; whether the branches of his trees shoot out abruptly in right angles from their trunks, or follow each other with only a gentle inclination. All of these circumstances contribute to the general character of the work, whether it be of the elegant, or of the more sublime kind.''

Young Turner's mind must have been filled with speculations such as these as the new century began. No doubt he was intrigued by aesthetic and philosophical ideas of all kinds, but also absorbed in projects that monopolized his time. Ruskin would have us believe that this is why he spent the whole of 1796 cooped up in his studio. The following year, however, Turner set out once again, this time on tours of Yorkshire, Northumberland, and the Lake District, scouring the countryside for fresh impressions. After so many months of unremitting work and strenuous effort to comply with academic standards, did he feel a need for breathing space, a dose of infinity, an urge to refresh himself by making sketches and watercolors in a relatively free, relaxed setting? Even diligence and steadfastness of purpose have their limits.(1)

This respite was short–lived, however, and Turner resumed his quest. His sketchbooks indicate that the work of Richard Wilson intrigued him at this time, and to get a firsthand view of things he traveled through Wilson's native North Wales ''in search of Richard Wilson's birthplace.'' (letter to Hawksworth Fawkes, December 27, 1847.) According to Andrew Wilton, both the *Academical* and Wilson sketchbooks display ''a particular concern with medium and are of blue paper washed over with a red-brown tone. The drawings are in a variety of media: pen and ink, chalks, watercolour, body-colour, all used in combinations that are unexpected and highly original.'' He went on to study the work of Joseph Vernet, but soon realized he had little use for Vernet's dry, clinical style. However, Turner also examined the paintings of Jacques-Philippe de Loutherbourg, the Alsatian–born designer of stage sets and devoté *extraordinaire* of theatrical perspective and illusion, as well as the effects of moonlight obtained by Joseph Wright of Derby. His thirst for knowledge spurred him to probe works that held the promise of unusual approaches or new insights, then to adapt and rework them in a way that might invest his own, still tentative efforts with greater conviction.(2)

This was Turner's first brush with what we refer to today as pictorial ''quotation.'' Although concealed to varying degrees, imitation was a practice he freely indulged in, and the list of painters he ''borrowed'' from or even (ill. 19) plagiarized over the years was long indeed. The earliest instance was *Aeneas and the Sibyl, Lake Avernus,* which probably dates from 1798. Sir Richard Colt Hoare, who owned Wilson's *Lake Nemi,* suggested that Turner paint a companion piece; the artist therefore felt entitled to copy both Wilson's style and subject. It should be emphasized that there was nothing reprehensible about this sort of thing at the time. Indeed, permission to imitate other painters had come from no less an authority than Reynolds himself, who declared in his first discourse to the Royal Academy in 1769; ''I would chiefly recommend that an implicit obedience to the *Rules of Art,* as established by the practice of the great masters, should be exacted from the *young* students. That those models, which have passed the approbation of ages, should be considered by them as perfect and infallible guides; as subjects for their imitation, not their criticism.'' Though not exhibited, *Aeneas and the Sibyl* marked Turner's first venture into ''polished'' painting in the classical tradition. The spirit of Claude weighs heavily here, especially in the way Turner's allegorical figures are blended in with the general contours of the composition.

This method of borrowing and recombining techniques and approaches soon bore fruit. Working with oils led Turner to modify his handling of watercolors, as his work from this period attests. ''Greater tonal range and sonority,'' as Wilton notes, ''can be obtained by working up towards highlights from a dark ground than by increasing the density of transparent pigments on white paper.'' He was still wary of too much light in the foreground, in compliance with Reynolds's recommendation. *The Refectory of Kirkstall Abbey, Yorkshire* is a study in (ill.23) which Turner experimented with sharply contrasting light and dark colors. The darkness enveloping the vaults is interrupted by a shaft of light from the left, only to reappear farther to the right in the form of half–tones; our eyes finally come to rest at the brightest area of the composition, a pastoral vista glimpsed through a break in the wall. The gradation of tone, albeit structured with utmost care, is neither ponderous nor strained.

With Ely and Salisbury cathedrals as his models, Turner drew a series of large watercolors (almost all of them (ill. 22) measure 65 by 50 cm.) for Sir Richard Colt Hoare. Here he developed and honed his ability to achieve picturesque effects. Furthermore, they gave him a chance to display his knowledge of architecture and the remarkable ease with which he could distribute light. Each time Turner lengthens or deepens a space, he alters our point of view, sends a signal to the viewer and guides him with consummate control. Certainly the artist does not spare us details, but there is nothing gratuitous about them, either; they ''make sense'' within the overall design. As he proceeded from one watercolor to the next, he varied volumes and lighting in ways that stimulate the viewer's imagination while still conveying the greatest possible amount of information about the places being depicted. The size of Turner's ''cathedral'' watercolors is commensurate with their subjects—grandiose specimens of Gothic architecture whose carved tracery held an entire generation spellbound in nostalgic reverie.

Durham Cathedral, from the river (1799)

The title of the first historical painting Turner sent to the annual exhibition of the Royal Academy is worthy of a document from a national archive: *The Battle of the Nile, at 10 o'clock, When the L'Orient Blew Up, from the Station of the Gunboats between the Battery and the Castle of Aboukir.* Although the painting itself is lost, information about it led Andrew Wilton to make two observations in his massive book on Turner. First, *The Battle of the Nile* was taken from contemporary history, for the incident took place in 1798. Second, ''...the inspiration must have been the sea-battles of Benjamin West and, perhaps more seriously, of Jacques-Philippe de Loutherbourg.'' It so happens that in 1792 Benjamin West succeeded Sir Joshua Reynolds as president of the Royal Academy and was still in office at the time of *The Battle of the Nile.* Perhaps it was cause-and-effect; perhaps sheer coincidence: in 1799 Turner was elected an Associate Member of the Royal Academy. He was twenty-four years old. Scarcely nine years had elapsed since he first sent work to an Academy exhibition. His ambition and diligence had paid off at last. He was on the right path, the path of respect and reputation. No longer able to ignore the call of his career, Turner left his parents' house and moved into more spacious quarters at 64 Harley Street. It was around this time that the artist's liaison with Sarah Danby began.

Turner's interest in Greco-Roman and biblical mythology, which first surfaced in 1798 with *Aeneas and the Sibyl, Lake Avernus,* continued with huge canvases depicting the fifth and tenth plagues of Egypt. The former was exhibited at the Royal Academy the year after his nomination, the latter in 1802. Whether it was simply to show what he was capable of achieving, or to prove that his talent could rival that of his colleagues, the fact remains that these two paintings marked a new phase in Turner's style. There is every reason to believe that each work Turner sent to the annual exhibition of the Royal Academy was carefully pondered and calculated to produce a certain effect, but he also wanted to help the viewer to better appreciate what he was attempting to depict or demonstrate. Probably Turner's entire career was a mingling of art and artifice. Within him lay dormant a man of the theater. After all, doesn't the composition of a painting involve ''staging'' of sorts, especially when its meaning is extended and enhanced by poetic allusion?

In 1798, the Royal Academy allowed painters to append quotations from poems to their titles; Turner, for his part, made frequent and often liberal use of them. His own earlier ventures into verse had yielded engaging, if not altogether felicitous results. Scattered throughout his sketchbooks we find a few lines here, a couplet there, the usual transports of love. Later on, however, he embarked on a much more ambitious project whose title, *The Fallacies of Hope,* may have come to the painter as he read Thomas Campbell's *The Pleasures of Hope* (which he finally illustrated in 1837). In it he developed the themes that were to haunt him his entire life: disillusionment and disappointment, the decrepitude of old age, the rotting away that comes with death, lust for gold, the lure of ambition. Although critics almost unanimously condemn his literary efforts for their mediocrity, and even if, in the estimation of contemporaries and posterity alike, his poems have an air of absurdity about them, they still attest to Turner's sincere desire to express himself more gracefully and his genuine need to give free rein to his feelings. Perhaps this outpouring of poetry was nothing more than a fashion, perhaps not. The fact remains that Turner did not see it as a source of conflict. Indeed, it reminds us of what may be a peculiarly English outlook, the tendency to feel painting, poetry, literature and nature as all part of the same surging desire to get closer to the ineffable or the unknown.

Since Turner drew on the Bible for his *Fifth Plague of Egypt* and *Tenth Plague of Egypt,* he decided to quote directly (ill. 20, 21) (ill. 20) from the scriptures, specifically, Exodus IX: 23 and 29–30. The dramatic themes of hailstorms and death gave him the chance to unite, in the guise of history, ravaged nature and the wrath of the Almighty, the timelessness of awe-inspiring architecture and the instability of life and human suffering. The painter mustered the entire arsenal of his youthful talent. In *The Fifth Plague of Egypt*, rain and hail sweep down on the land of the Pharoahs with a vengeance. Ominous flashes of light dart across a raging sky, crash down on a distant pyramid, and illuminate a dying horse in the foreground. The heavens crackling with sulfur, a countryside laid waste by the wrath of God—it smacks of theatrics. The outstretched horse ''spotlighted'' in a glistening circle of pale color all too readily brings to mind the way still-life artists traditionally placed a knife on a table in order to establish the various distances. The shaft of light piercing the darkness indicates how profound Rembrandt's influence had been. In any event, the seething atmosphere of *The Fifth Plague of Egypt*—the subject is actually the seventh plague—must have appealed to William Beckford, the brilliant, illustrious, and fabulously wealthy author of *Vathek*, who purchased the painting.

(ill. 21) Turner's *Tenth Plague of Egypt*, though equally dramatic, shows more in the way of classical restraint. It seems that the only reason he placed the women mourning their dead children in the foreground was to give meaning to the grief-stricken fortress city behind them. Jean-Jacques Mayoux incisively notes that ''in terms of effect, [these buildings] are more pre-Martin than post-Poussin.'' Hard-edged and oppressive, the city stands in marked contrast to the brutal, windswept landscape in *The Fifth Plague of Egypt*. The two-year interval between the paintings had given Turner the chance to study Poussin, and he learned his lesson well. The arrangement and play of forms, the range of chromatic harmonies and contrasts, even the frontality of the composition—everything points to a scrupulous observance of the canons laid down by Poussin, a painter who was invariably cited as a paragon of that ''noblest'' branch of art, history painting. Although critics took notice of *The Tenth Plague of Egypt* and acknowledged its strong points, no one stepped forward to buy it.

Turner's close study of the Poussins at Bridgewater House had been preceded by an encounter that was to prove far more decisive in terms of the future development of his work. When he was at William Beckford's in the spring of 1799, he saw the two Claudes that Beckford had just acquired from the Altieri collection. The experience shook him to the core, and the painter is reported to have said on seeing *The Sacrifice of Apollo*, ''it seemed to be beyond the power of imitation'' (Finberg). Turner considered this an art so flawless, so consummate, so close to what he himself was probably trying to achieve, that he felt he could never reach the same level. Consequently, he believed it necessary to continue improving his technique before he could attempt anything like it. Rightly or wrongly, Poussin intimidated him less, but what he had learned from Claude would one day result in as Finberg puts it, ''a new character in his profession.''

In his biographical sketch of the painter (published in 1805), Edward Dayes observed ''[Turner] may be considered as a striking instance of how much may be gained by industry, if accompanied with temperance, even without the assistance of a master. The way he acquired his professional powers was by borrowing, where he could, a drawing or picture to copy from;...'' Today, his favorable evaluation cannot help striking us as rather ambiguous. Nevertheless, sensible, dutiful pupils like Turner, who put their craft above all else, who put great store by ''industry'' and ''temperance,'' as well as ''professional powers'' forged by borrowing or adaptation, had places waiting for them in the ranks of the Royal Academy. Its mission, after all, was to maintain order and tradition. Turner was elected a full member of the Academy on February 12, 1802, at the age of twenty–seven.

18. MOONLIGHT, A STUDY AT MILLBANK
R.A. 1797 — Oil on mahogany panel, 31.5 x 40.5 cm
Tate Gallery, London.

19. AENEAS AND THE SIBYL, LAKE AVERNUS
c. 1798 — Oil on canvas, 76.5 x 98.5 cm
Tate Gallery, London.

20. THE FIFTH PLAGUE OF EGYPT
    R.A. 1800 — Oil on canvas, 124 x 183 cm
    Indianapolis Museum of Art.

21. THE TENTH PLAGUE OF EGYPT
    R.A. 1802 — Oil on canvas, 142 x 263 cm
    Tate Gallery, London.

22. CHAPTER — HOUSE, SALISBURY
R.A. 1801 — Pencil and watercolor, 66 x 50.8 cm
Victoria and Albert Museum, London.

23. STUDY FOR THE REFECTORY OF KIRKSTALL ABBEY
c. 1798 — Aquatint and mezzotint, 16 x 24 cm
British Museum, London.

24. KILGARREN CASTEL
c. 1798 — Watercolor, 26.7 x 36.5 cm
City Art Gallery, Manchester.

25. INTERNAL OF A COTTAGE, A STUDY AT ELY
R.A. 1796 — Watercolor over pencil, 19.8 x 27.1 cm
British Museum, London.

26. ABERGAVENNY BRIDGE, MONMOUTHSHIRE, CLEARING UP
AFTER A SHOWERY DAY
R.A. 1799 — Watercolor, 41.3 x 76 cm
Victoria and Albert Museum, London.

27. STUDY FOR PEMBROKE CASTLE
   c. 1801 — Pen and ink, with brown wash and some gouache on blue paper,
   13 x 21 cm
   British Museum, London.

28. CAERNARVON CASTLE, NORTH WALES
   R.A. 1800 — Watercolor, 66.3 x 99.4 cm
   British Museum, London.

III. HIGH ART: SWITZERLAND, THE LOUVRE, LIBER STUDIORUM

"Love for that distant horizon, love for that mortal horizon, is an attainment of Baroque and, in the end, romantic art."

Eugenio d'Ors

Turner was irresistibly drawn to the sea his entire life, and it in turn mirrored his changing style. At first he was content simply to describe the sea—now tranquil, now buffeted by ranging storms, now studded with fishermen's boats or brigantines—but it evolved into a symbolic stage for human passions.

Such is the case with the two massive paintings he exhibited at the Royal Academy in 1801 and 1802, despite their seemingly straightforward titles: *Dutch Boats in a Gale: Fishermen Endeavouring to Put their Fish on Board* and *Ships Bearing Up for Anchorage* (better known by the names of the individuals who commissioned them, *The Bridgewater Sea Piece* and *The Egremont Sea Piece*). When viewed side by side, these impressive compositions offer the viewer's imagination a wide range of "sublime" associations. Braving the perils of the sea in order to survive, the fishermen in *Dutch Boats in a Gale* are locked in a pitched battle with the elements as a brooding sky hovers overhead. The water line is disturbing proof that the heavy swells are overtaxing the weary little craft. A triangle of light all around the boat echoes its taut, triangular sail. The painter fills the foreground and middle distance with an exuberant evocation of a choppy sea flecked with windswept whitecaps. To be sure, he was still doing his utmost to follow in the tradition of the acknowledged masters of the genre, namely, seventeenth-century Dutch painters, but the fiery lighting effects and high emotional pitch of *Dutch Boats in a Gale* show that Turner was, perhaps reluctantly, veering away from them.

The assembled ships in *The Egremont Sea Piece* seem to be awaiting a command or signal from destiny. Some have (ill. 30) their sails set, others have them taken in; they appear to be lost or hesitant as they confront the immensity of the formidable sea. Immensity—this yearning to be free from spatial restrictions had already surfaced in eighteenth-century England in the garden designs of William Kent. Formal boundaries were pulled down or rooted out, the better to confuse order, now made to look uncontrived, and the disorderliness of nature. Henceforth the garden could be appreciated in terms of a conflict between freedom and authority. Stone and brick gave way to "ha-has," enclosing moats whose name evokes the startled stroller's reaction to them. Of course, the restrictions were still there, but illusion and imagination were given ample opportunity to work their wonders.

"The close connection between the soul and the garden evolved into an equally intimate link between the soul and nature," notes Marie–Madeleine Martinet. "The parks of the latter part of the [eighteenth] century— such as Fonthill, William Beckford's Wiltshire estate—were designed to evoke nature in its untamed state." In a moment of supreme extravagance, Beckford had the architect Wyatt build a Gothic abbey, but the central tower collapsed in 1825.

The master of Fonthill commissioned Turner to execute five watercolors (seven, by Farington's reckoning), and they were exhibited at the Royal Academy in 1800. Unfortunately, they have not held up well over the years. These sweeping landscapes and gently rolling hills are still very much in the tradition of Claude. Although Turner glossed over details, he was careful to build up forms with tiny brushstrokes; his preliminary sketches for this series give us an idea of the painstaking process by which he attempted to create atmospheric effects solely through color. The approach he adopted for the "Fonthill" watercolors was still fresh in his mind when, taking advantage of the short–lived Peace of Amiens, he set sail for the Continent on July 15, 1802. Actually, the methodical Turner had begun preparing for this journey as far back as 1789, familiarizing himself with French, making inquiries about guides, pinpointing stops along the route. Above all he longed to see the mountains. And where could one better contemplate mountains in their boundless, dramatic majesty than in Switzerland? Of course, Turner was hardly the first to heed the call of the Alps: for some fifty years, hordes of English painters and tourists had been descending on Switzerland in search of emotion, the picturesque, and the sublime.

If Turner felt ready to depict this age–old spectacle in watercolor, where emphasis is not so much on form as on chromatic effect, perhaps it was because he had already come to grips with the problem of rendering light and

Chateau de St. Michael, Bonneville, Savoy (R.A. 1803)

shade in their starkest terms. He had returned from his tour of Scotland in 1801 with approximately sixty drawings in pencil, chalk, and white gouache on paper washed with ''India Ink and tobacco water'' (Farington). Dubbed by Ruskin the ''Scottish Pencils,'' these rather tedious monochrome exercises honed Turner's ability to structure great sweeps of space and sharpened his eye for overlapping visual planes.

The sketchbook that Turner filled during his Swiss travels allows us to retrace the artist's itinerary. On his return trip he ran into Farington in Paris and told him that the trees were ''bad for a painter…—fragments and precipices very romantic and strikingly grand,'' and that ''the Country on the whole surpasses Wales, and Scotland too'' (quoted in Finberg).

There is something oppressive and overwhelming about the way Turner arranged his volumes, his light and dark tones, in *St. Hugues Denouncing Vengeance on the Shepherd of Cormayeur, in the Valley of D'Aoste* (R. A. 1803). The contrast between an appealing, picturesque scene and a ''sublime'' atmosphere of dread is designed to ''harmonize'' the characters with their natural setting. Balanced opposites are also the key to *The Châteaux de St. Michael, Bonneville, Savoy,* Turner's first attempt to depict mountains in oils. The vista to the left would have resulted in a lopsided distribution of volumes had Turner not been careful to interrupt the shadowy area with a piercing square of light and softened the effect with a matching pair of sloping mountain crests. The great cumulus clouds scudding across a washed-out sky add a note of uncertainty to the moment captured by the painter's brush, but the overall brightness of the atmosphere preserves the stability of this daring composition.

(ill. 44) Though *The Mer de Glace, with Blair's Hut* is a comparatively small watercolor, Turner's aim was to bring the viewer face-to-face with the immensity and terrifying grandeur of glaciers. Between the ice formations in the foreground and a background bristling with snow-covered peaks, we see a dark, triangular area that runs along an abruptly interrupted diagonal. It is a glistening and awesome evocation of geological forces; the iridescent whites seem to crunch and crack before our very eyes. The arrangement of whites, carefully structured forms, and vast, unbroken sweep of space give us an idea of what Turner's feelings must have been at the time: now uplifted, now terrified by a natural spectacle of jolting intensity. As a concession to the rules of the genre, the painter made sure to temper the emotional impact of the scene by adding a place of refuge and safety—a distant hut. Like all of Turner's ''alpine'' watercolors from this period, *The Mer de Glace* owes its extraordinary effect to consummate craftsmanship. The technique he adopted for this series was highly original, if not unique: he would superimpose bold areas of wash on white paper—they cold be quickly absorbed with a sponge or blotter—then use a virtually dry brush, adding fine hatches of color for texture and scraping his legendary ''eagle-claw of a thumbnail'' against the paper. This hard-won vituosity attests to the fundamental, almost ritualistic complicity that must have developed between Turner and his medium, as well as between his own mind and heart.

St. Huges Denouncing Vengeance on the Shepherd of Cormayer, in the Valley of d'Aoste (R.A. 1803)

(ill. 42) The *Mer de Galce* was bought by Walter Fawkes, who, in 1803, had already purchased *Glacier and Source of the Arvenon, Going Up the Mer de Glace,* a majestic watercolor that marked the beginning of the largest collection of Turners in England, including everything from the tour of Switzerland. Thus blossomed the painter's enduring friendship with the proprietor of Farnley Hall, near Leeds (Yorkshire). Turner was regular guest at Fawkes's
(ill. 45) estate, where he painted an important series of watercolors, probably between 1815 and 1819. Fanciful works, these—there is even a lyrical evocation of the splendid main building with its garden and grounds, quite unlike the detailed renderings of the castle interior. Utterly devoid of human presence, the main rooms are recorded with the kind of dispassionate detail that photography would soon make commonplace.

Turner's landing at Calais in 1802 had been a brush with disaster. He harked back to the incident on two different
(ill. 31) occasions, first in 1803 with *Calais Pier, with French Poissards Preparing for Sea: An English Packet Arriving* and again in
(ill. 29) 1805 with *The Shipwreck: Fishing Boats Endeavouring to Rescue the Crew.* In both instances Turner took his subject from everyday life and raised it to a ''sublime'' level. To struggle desperately with the unbridled elements—such is the tragic plight of man the painter depicts here. The headless French fishermen of *Calais Pier,* bottle of spirits in hand, are doing nothing to prevent their being swept away by the gale, whereas the stalwart English sailors in *The Shipwreck* are doing all they can to save human lives despite the heaving sea. Turner was to return time and again to, as Ruskin put it, the theme of ''utmost anxiety and distress.'' *The Shipwreck* is probably the first large-scale marine in which Turner's powers of invention really began to shine through.

In official art circles, the two paintings were greeted with sharp criticism. Benjamin West, Henry Fuseli, and the Beau Brummell of pictorial elegance, Sir George Beaumont, were unanimous in their disapproval. They all deplored the style as ''too little attended to—too undefined.'' These reservations notwithstanding, Lord Gower offered to purchase it (without success, it turned out, for the thought the asking price too high). As for *The Shipwreck,* Benjamin West thought it tended to imbecility (Lindsay), while Hoppner dismissed Turner's pictures as ''rank, crude, and disordered.'' Indeed, the fruits of Turner's fiery imagination hardly fit in with the canons promulgated by the Academy. And so the painter found himself confronted with the attitude that so often greets originality and freshness; rejection.

Charles Turner (1777–1857) was the first to purchase the right to reproduce a mezzotint of the painting. Although the engravings were promised for 1805, they were not completed and put on the market until 1807. The results were superb. Thus was launched a lifelong association between the two Turners, one that suffered its share of contretemps and injury. The many advantages to be derived from this kind of activity—additional income, publicity—were all too obvious to the painter, and the two of them began work on a major undertaking, the *Liber Studiorum* (1).

The Destruction of Sodom (c. 1805)

Turner recorded his reactions to the great works of the masters in a sketchbook labeled *Studies in the Louvre*. Alert and clearheaded, he scrutinized them with a technician's eye. He was critical of Rubens's *The Rainbow*, which Reynolds considered an exemplary painting, but added that "the colour is sublime. It is natural—it is what a creative mind must be imprest with by sympathy and horror." Elsewhere, however, he notes that Rubens "threw around his tints like a bunch of flowers." He found Jacob van Ruisdael disappointing, but copied him anyway. Poussin left him stunned. The *Gathering of Manna*," Finberg notes, "he regarded as the grandest system of light and shade in the collections." He also made copious notes about Rembrandt and analyzed Titian's style. Curiously enough, he had nothing at all to say about Claude Lorrain, even though the works in the Louvre are among Claude's finest in terms of sheer luminosity.

Over the next few years, the observations and drawings he made in the "Louvre" sketchbook were to inspire, directly or indirectly, works in which Poussinesque mythology serves as a pretext for landscapes that blend observation of nature with carefully thought-out, at times nightmarish themes. These include *The Deluge, The Destruction of Sodom*, the disturbing *Goddess of Discord Choosing the Apple of Contention in the Garden of the Hesperides*, (ill.48) and *Apollo and Python*. In *Holy Family*, closely adapted from Titian, Turner reversed traditional iconography in (ill.50,33) spite of his allegiance to the code of "high art." Over the ages, painters treating this subject have strained their ingenuity to focus the viewer's eyes on the child. In this case, Jesus looks up at an affectionate, admiring Mary; mother and child are merged into a skillfully arranged triangle of lighter color. Perhaps this break with tradition was Turner's heartrending way of expressing his longing for the maternal closeness he never knew. He had been effectively cut off from his emotionally disturbed mother at an early age, and it was around the time of *Holy Family* that she became ill in Bethlem Hospital, where remained until 1804.

Turner's silence about the Claudes he saw in the Louvre is all the more puzzling in that he must have spent long hours mulling over his style and, indeed, painted as though competing with the renowned French landscapist of the seventeenth century.

In 1803, a few months after his return from the Continent, the Royal Academy received *The Festival upon the* (ill.34) *Opening of the Vintage at Mâcon*, an idyllic, orderly landscape complete with a garland of nymphlike grape–gatherers. The sweeping panorama is punctuated by trees with full, spreading boughs. Like a horse clearing hurdles, our eyes follow the winding river, leap over the bridge, proceed from middle to far distance and out to the horizon and the boundless sky. The intense glare of the setting sun is filtered through an enveloping "womb" of mist and cloud. Although the *Vintage at Mâcon* is a textbook example of classical composition—browns for the foreground, greens for the middle distance, blues for the far distance—Turner painted it on an unprimed canvas, resulting in exceptionally vivid colors that were a conspicuous departure from the norm. "The subject of Mâcon," Sir George Beaumont remarked to Farington, "was borrowed from Claude, but the colouring forgotten."

Copy of Titian's *The Entombment* (1802)

The reviews came as a cruel blow to Turner, for they shattered the splendid image he had had of himself (for that matter, which we all tend to have of ourselves). When growing resistance within the ranks of both the General Assembly and the Council of the Royal Academy turned the hanging of his pictures into a source of contention, the painter made a daring decision. In 1804, he extended the first floor of his Harley Street residence and turned it into a gallery of his own. Each spring for some twelve years he invited the public to come and view his work in the gallery, although he continued to take part in Academy exhibitions. He acquired a house at 47 Queen Anne Street and, after encroaching on neighboring houses, extensive remodeling, and considerable maneuvering, he ended up with more spacious quarters that were better suited to his goals and aspirations.

Wan, diffused light and unusual perspective are what give *Sun Rising through Vapour: Fishermen Cleaning and* (ill.32) *Selling Fish* its eerie, otherworldly, sea–green pallor. The busy fishermen might be characters out of a Bruegel painting. Turner believed that his treatment of this slice of everyday life—it was to remain one of his favorite works—would expose the artificiality of Claude and thereby show his own talent to advantage.

There can be little doubt that *Dido Building Carthage, Crossing the Brook,* and *The Decline of the Carthaginian Empire* (ill.55,52,57) were all further attempts to compete with Claude, but they were also Turner's way of displaying his comparative independence and superiority. For the two "Carthage" canvases, he borrowed from his rival all the usual arrangements of forms, but was careful to invest every detail with special meaning or metaphorical overtones. The entire composition is flooded with a golden light that skirts the entablatures and tinges the smallest column. The devices and "sets" are pure Claude, but the desired effect is different. All of Turner's characters—queen, architects, and fishermen alike—are living, breathing individuals who contribute to the dynamics of the scene, whether overseeing the building of a city, taking part in the actual construction, or cleaning fish and selling it at auction.

Turner's persistent, almost obsessive tendency to measure himself against Claude ought not to overshadow his work in other branches of painting. Since his attempts at heroic art and the grand manner had brought him nothing but scorn, he set out to win the public over with genre painting, which was very much in vogue at the (ill.38) time. The palette of *The Blacksmith's Shop* consists of a subtle range of yellows; the brushwork is lively, piquant, akin to the light, transparent touch he had learned to use to such advantage. The lengthy title, more befitting at (ill.37) treatise on economics that a painting, affords us a glimpse into the way Turner's mind worked. *The Garreteer's Petition*, painted on a mahogany panel that happened to be close at hand, might well bring to mind one of Rembrandt's ''philosophers''; both display exceptionally refined shading and place the light source at the left. But the feeling of Turner's composition is far less intense, less introspective. The subject (the accompanying poem in the catalogue informs us) is a poet calling upon the Muse to help him finish his work, but the pose he is striking seems affected.

Mountains, whether in Switzerland or more exotic settings, crop up time and again in Turner's oeuvre. His (ill.35,36) *Eruption of Mt. Soufrière*, painted after a sketch drawn by an eyewitness, and *Vesuvius in Eruption* gave him the chance to satisfy his taste for catastropic events and to depict an awe inspiring moment of geological convulsion with reds, deep or brilliant blues, and harsh yellows. In both works, the darkness is slashed by terrifying bursts of molten lava.

(ill.47) Surging violence could just as easily take the form of ice and snow, and in *The Fall of an Avalanche in the Grisons*, they engulf everything that lies in their path. Ruskin marveled at the enormous boulder, captured the instant before it smashes into a pathetic little cabin. The composition as a whole is focused on a pair of intersecting diagonals that form a kind of gigantic multiplication sign. Oddly enough, instead of ''freezing'' the action, the painter quietly succeeds in making the awesome downward flow and the unsteadiness of the rocks seem that much more immediate and intense. The various distances are articulated with boldnesss and vigor, while the artist's handling of white—now misty, now laid on in icy, stabbing strokes—is nothing short of marvelous. Compared to the avalanche that Jacques–Philippe de Loutherbourg had depicted (and which Turner had seen at Lord Egremont's), Turner's version bursts with a spirit, an enthusiasm, a feeling for nature that far surpasses the theatrical gestures of de Loutherbourg's peasants.

Jacques-Philippe de Loutherbourg: An Avalanche in the Alps (c. 1803)

In every facet of his art, Turner worked at a feverish pace and channeled all of his energy into satisfying the grueling demands of his craft. However, it was during this period—perhaps the only period of his life—that he loved and was loved in return. Though not an irrefutable proof of affection, Sarah Danby gave birth to two daughters; it is likely that Turner was the father. But most of his time was taken up with remodeling his house, painting, engraving, and traveling. At the request of George Cooke, he toured Kent, Devon, and Cornwall for a series entitled *Views in the Southern Coast of England*.

In 1807 Turner was named Professor of Perspective at the Academy—this artist who, when the opportunity presented itself, could take such liberties with perspective! Although his expertise in the field was unimpeachable, he was hardly cut out for such a position. Turner was a poor speaker; his cockney accent was as strong as ever, and his arguments were often difficult to follow. He procrastinated until 1811, when he finally mounted the rostrum and delivered the first of what proved to be a series of unsuccessful and unpopular lectures. His diagrams and drawings, which *did* capture his listeners' attention, show how carefully he prepared each of his classes. So intense was his craving for recognition that he could not pass up the honor of being elected a professor of the Royal Academy. This institution seems to have had a twofold meaning for Turner. It was at once a substitute for the loving and beloved mother he never had, and the ''father'' responsible for upholding tradition.

(ill.51) Turner's first significant attempt to throw off the yoke of convention came with *Snow Storm: Hannibal and his Army Crossing the Alps*. Although the action unfolding on canvas and the upheaval taking place within the artist were part of the same drama, it is likely that Turner himself was not fully aware of its meaning and implications.

29. THE SHIPWRECK
1805 — Oil on canvas, 171.5 x 241.5 cm
Tate Gallery, London.

30. SHIPS BEARING UP FOR ANCHORAGE
   ("THE EGREMONT SEA PIECE")
   R.A. 1802 — Oil on canvas, 119.5 x 180.3 cm
   H.M. Treasury and National Trust (Lord Egremont Collection),
   Petworth House, Sussex

31. CALAIS PIER, WITH FRENCH POISSARDS PREPARING
FOR SEA: AN ENGLISH PACKET ARRIVING
R.A. 1803 — Oil on canvas, 172 x 240 cm
National Gallery, London.

32. SUN RISING THROUGH VAPOUR: FISHERMEN CLEANING AND
SELLING FISH
R.A. 1807 – Oil on canvas, 134.5 x 179 cm

33. HOLY FAMILY
R.A. 1803 — Oil on canvas, 102 x 141.5 cm
Tate Gallery, London.

34. THE FESTIVAL UPON THE OPENING OF THE VINTAGE AT MÂCON
R.A. 1803 — Oil on canvas, 146 x 237.5 cm
City Art Galleries, Sheffield.

35. THE ERUPTION OF THE SOUFFRIER MOUNTAINS, IN THE IS-
LAND OF ST. VINCENT, AT MIDNIGHT, ON THE 30TH OF APRIL,
1812, FROM A SKETCH TAKEN AT THE TIME BY HUGH P. KEANE,
ESQ.
R.A. 1815 — Oil on canvas, 79.4 x 104.8 cm
University of Liverpool.

36. ERUPTION OF VESUVIUS
1817 — Watercolor and scraping-out, 28.6 x 39.7 cm
Yale Center for British Art, Paul Mellon Collection.

37. THE GARRETEER'S PETITION
R.A. 1809 — Oil on mahogany panel, 55 x 79 cm
Tate Gallery, London.

37.

38. COUNTRY BLACKSMITH DISPUTING UPON THE PRICE OF IRON,
AND THE PRICE CHARGED TO THE BUTCHER FOR SHOEING HIS
PONEY
R.A. 1807 — Oil on pine panel, 57.5 x 80.5 cm
Tate Gallery, London.

39. BOLTON ABBEY, YORKSHIRE
1809 — Watercolor and scraping-out, 27.8 x 39.5 cm
British Museum, London.

40. LOCH FYNE
1815 — Watercolor and some scraping-out, 27.8 x 38.8 cm
British Museum, London.

41. BONNEVILLE, SAVOY
   c. 1802 — Watercolor and white gouache, 21 x 47 cm
   Courtauld Institute of Art, London.

42. GLACIER AND SOURCE OF THE ARVERON,
   GOING UP TO THE MER DE GLACE
   R.A. 1803 — Watercolor, 68.5 x 101.5 cm
   Yale Center for British Art, Paul Mellon Collection.

43. THE CASTLE OF CHILLON
1809? — Watercolor and some scraping-out, 28.1 x 39.5 cm
British Museum, London.

44. MER DE GLACE, WITH BLAIR'S HUT
1806 — Watercolor, with some gouache, 27.4 x 38.9 cm
British Museum, London.

45. AT FARNLEY HALL (A FRONTISPIECE)
   1815 — Watercolor over pencil, with pen and ink and a little scratching-out,
   17.8 x 24.2 cm
   Ashmolean Museum, Oxford.

46. FRONTISPIECE FOR THE LIBER STUDIORUM
   c. 1811 — Engraving
   British Museum, London.

47. THE FALL OF AN AVALANCHE IN THE GRISONS (COTTAGE DESTROYED BY AN AVALANCHE) 1810 — Oil on canvas, 90 x 120 cm Tate Gallery, London.

48. THE GODDESS OF DISCORD CHOOSING THE APPLE OF
CONTENTION IN THE CARDEN OF THE HESPERIDES
1806 — Oil on canvas, 155 x 218.5 cm
Tate Gallery, London.

49. DIDO AND AENEAS
R.A. 1814 — Oil on canvas, 146 x 237.0 cm
Tate Gallery, London.

50. APOLLO AND PYTHON
R.A. 1811 — Oil on canvas, 145.5 x 237.5 cm
Tate Gallery, London.

51. SNOW STORM: HANNIBAL AND HIS ARMY CROSSING THE ALPS
   R.A. 1812 — Oil on canvas, 146 x 237.5 cm
   Tate Gallery, London.

IV. THE GRAND TOUR

"Raphael was not only the greatest of painters; he was handsome, he was kind, he was everything."

Ingres

We know that *Snow Storm: Hannibal and His Army Crossing the Alps* was inspired by a violent thunderstorm that an   (ill.51)
"entranced" Turner had observed while visiting with his friend, Walter Fawkes, at his estate in Yorkshire. Was it a sudden premonition or a sudden fulfillment of something he had been waiting for? Pointing to the sketches, he said to Fawkes's son, Hawkesworth, "There,…in two years you will see this again, and call it Hannibal Crossing the Alps!" As one of the drawings in the *Calais Pier* sketchbook attests, the subject did indeed stay fresh in his mind. Long in gestation, but probably executed in a vary brief space of time, this curiously original painting was a turning point in the artist's career. True, there had been cautious infractions of the Rules of Art in the past, but *Hannibal* marked a definitive break with traditions which Turner had, by and large, respected until then.

Historians agree that there were two sources for *Hannibal*, one literary, the other pictorial. Mrs. Radcliffe describes a similar scene in *The Mysteries of Udolfo* (1794), and John Robert Cozens had treated the same subject in a painting that is now lost. Turner himself is reported to have declared that Cozens's version of the Hannibal theme inspired him above all others. Although these sources certainly have their place in our discussion, it is more intriguing to consider the possibility that the subject struck a chord within the painter's soul. The destruction of Carthage— here was a theme that blended voluptuousness and punishment (perhaps, in Turner's case, punishment as a kind of voluptuousness). John Gage suggests that Turner may have been comparing Rome and Carthage on the one hand, and the conflict between England and France on the other. It was common analogy at the time, and the political overtones of *Hannibal* cannot be ruled out of our interpretation.

A tremendous storm is sweeping down on a jeering Hannibal, seated on an elephant in the middle distance, and a dark, teeming mass of soldiers bursting forth from a deep valley. In the foreground we see the soldiers plundering, killing, and raping with the same cruelty that Goya portrayed in *Los Desastres de la Guerra*. But the scope and pitch of violence here is of an entirely different order. In *Hannibal Crossing the Alps*, the elements are unleashing an immense vortex of thick, greenish smoke; eventually it splits apart to reveal a sinister orange sun that cannot dispel the mists hanging in the sky. The striking difference in scale between man and nature was a departure from traditional proportions, and this effective device was Turner's way of suggesting the Carthaginians' fate. The brushwork is bold, scraped with a knife. The blacks are intense; the whites congeal into heavy curtains of pattering sleet. Glimmering light in the distance reveals the fertile plains on which the army is destined to face destruction, not in the clash of arms, but in the luxurious indolence of Capua.

Hannibal Crossing the Alps shattered the sacrosanct laws of composition; the tranquility of classical arrangement has been replaced by a whirlwind of unprecedented enormity. A new, explosive—romantic—way of structuring space was surfacing in Turner's work, one that allowed greater fluidity of form. The visual planes seem to be obeying their own laws of movement as they glide over one another, straining to mesh. The overall impresson is one of violence, a feeling that man is caught up and tossed about in a whirlwind of terrestrial forces. Turner's swirling (womblike?) oval brings the viewer face–to–face with the unruliness of nature and, metaphorically, the turbulence of human passions. The painter had just discovered that he himself lay at the very heart of the whirlwind.

Despite *Hannibal*'s highly unconventional structure, critics reacted to it with the usual formulas of aesthetic evaluation. It was for them a terrifying, sublime evocation of nature, a demonstration of how "the sublime" could be evoked by darkness, by nature in all her dreadful, uncanny magnificence. There can be no denying all this, but behind the screen of "appreciation" lies the fact that, in the eyes of contemporaries, it had all the earmarks of novelty. Placed in historical context, we see that *Hannibal* was indeed a watershed in painting. An offshoot of humankind's undying tendency to the baroque, it speaks of the diabolical burden of destiny and of man's unquenchable longing for the infinite—that burning thirst that cannot be slaked.

Turner completed *Hannibal Crossing the Alps* seven years before his first trip to Italy, but in terms of overall design and its use of black as a color in its own right, it was the first, imperceptible crack in the career he had worked so diligently to forge. But he was slow in learning its lesson, and the process was to continue for many years. Turner clung to tradition. For all the liberties he took and for all his departures from accepted procedures, the final break would be long in coming.

Turner had every reason to choose this moment for his Grand Tour (1). Napoleon had been in exile since 1815, and Europeans once again enjoyed freedom of movement. The magical hold that the sun-drenched countries of the South had on the British soul was as powerful as ever. But Turner also must have been drawn by his admiration for Italian art and artists, for Claude Lorrain, for Poussin and his brother-in-law Gaspard Dughet, for Salvator Rosa.

The painter was exceptionally well prepared for his stint abroad. In 1798 he had painted an Italian landscape after a drawing by Richard Colt Hoare; in 1818 he agreed to do eighteen watercolors from pencil drawings that James Hakewill had made in Italy. They appeared two years later as *A Picturesque Tour of Italy.* The celebrated cities they (ill. 36) portray—Florence, Naples, Rome—must have sent Turner's imagination spinning and whetted his appetite to see the country firsthand. The cordial individual who commissioned the series took the role of guide, pointing out places of interest and monuments worth visiting, all of which Turner recorded in a sketchbook he labeled *Route to Rome.* The painter set out from London in August, 1819. Egged on by curiosity, he resolved from the moment he left to assimilate and store away as much information as possible.

Of the twenty or so sketchbooks Turner filled during this trip (nearly all of them measure 11 by 18 cm.), nineteen are devoted to Italy. They are cram-full of notes and on-the-spot pencil sketches, with particular attention given to the costumes of peasants and "Venetian Merchants." The *Tivoli and Rome, Vatican Fragments,* and *St. Peter's* sketchbooks teem with elaborate studies and copies of paintings, sculpture, antiques, and monuments. He sketched like a man possessed; his keen observer's eye took in everything. Only four of the sketchbooks include watercolors, while a fifth, labeled *Skies,* is a group of washes shimmering with delicate color. In many others he began by washing the sheets of paper with gray, then scraping to expose the white surface, a procedure he had already tried out in Switzerland and in 1817 during his journey along the Rhine. Usually he worked with pencil, but now and again he switched to pen and ink for details or when he could proceed at a more leisurely pace in his room. The prepared sheets lent themselves to an often overly meticulous depiction of atmospheric effects. The sun, the moon, iridescent rainbows—light in Turner's hands took on an uncommon, highly personal kind of palpability. These watercolors (some have gouache added) are startlingly "tactile"; they seem to breach the gap between sight and touch.

Apparently the pace at which Turner worked varied considerably. At this juncture, however, there was no technical difficulty his virtuosity could not overcome. He worked freely, instinctively; what mattered was not to obtain a certain effect, to capture something that was neither "accurate" nor contrived, but sensed, intuited. Turner was forty-four years old, and by this time he had matured into a versatile and resourceful craftsman. His hands did the bidding of his will, sorting out and deciding what would dissolve, burst, or gush forth on the piece of paper before him.

White paper is especially well-suited to capturing ethereal light, and this is what Turner used for his miraculous (ill. 63) watercolor, *Venice: San Giorgio Maggiore from the Dogana.* Both sea and sky take on a greenish cast that is very close to turquoise. Modulations of this tone result in darker areas in the form of rectangles, a vertical, and a few gently curving lines. The silhouette of the city in the distance has been reduced to a single pale line veiled in pearly mist and devoid of relief. Amid this supple play of color shines a pure, gossamer, crystalline light, a light that, even here, had already begun to consume and slash into forms. They very directness of Turner's technique smacks of rediscovered innocence, a rediscovered Venice. This watercolor made off with some of her light and fashioned her anew on a sheet of paper. Venice had never existed before; she came into being the moment the artist, oblivious of artistic hierarchies, applied the first dab of color. She bursts forth, fresh and vital, each time we look at it.

What occurred that day was not unlike the breathless admiration of love. In 1832 Delacroix experienced the same kind of elation when he discovered the intoxicating colors of the Near East. Klee was likewise dazed during his stay in Tunisia in 1914. "Color possesses me," he wrote in his *Diary.* "I no longer have to seek it out. It possesses me forever, I know it....Color and I are inseparable. I am a painter."

Turner, too, no longer needed to seek it out. He came into being the moment this watercolor did. It was the first time he had not confused light with lighting, and he would never do so again. The aftershocks of his discovery were to be felt in four other watercolors, all devoted to Venice. The city is enveloped in an opalescent light: only a few blobs of ocher for boats rocking to and fro, a streak of transparent red and a translucent blue gray for the first glimmers of sunrise. However, Turner did not let himself get carried away by the ecstasy of revelation. He proceeded through this uncharted poetic terrain with caution. But he was making the transition from formula art to something more akin to enchantment.

This jolting discovery did not trigger a burst of feverish activity. Turner needed time to sort out and clarify his thoughts. He knew what he was doing, but he still had to assimilate the experience, perhaps even decide whether or not to pursue it. We might better trace this process if we take a backward glance at the previous few years of Turner's career. In 1815 he had exhibited *Crossing the Brook* at the Royal Academy; in 1818, *Raby Castle, the Seat of the Earl of Darlington.*

Along with *Dido and Aeneas, Dido Building Carthage,* and *The Decline of the Carthaginian Empire, Crossing the Brook* is (ill. 55, 57, 52) generally considered a high point of the first half of the painter's career. The foreground of the landscape is hemmed in on either side by trees, but opens onto a panoramic view of the countryside. The sky takes up fully half of the entire canvas. The aerial perspective in the far distance is perfectly controlled and executed with utmost refinement. The composition proper consists of a semicircle for the main scene and a triangle formed by the cascading foliage to the right. The latter is counterbalanced by a clump of lofty trees with curving boughs; their position and carefully calculated height make them a focal point of the arrangement. The bridge in the middle distance, with its graduated arches, forms a line that echoes the horizon and lends a sense of calm and serenity to the composition as a whole. The original palette of yellows, greens, and browns underneath the varnish has become almost monochromatic today. The two girls at the water's edge—convention dictated that a landscape be ''justified'' by human figures—are thought to be Evelina and Georgiana, the illegitimate daughters Turner probably had by Sarah Danby. Based on sketches he had made in Devonshire, *Crossing the Brook* is a perfect example of how Turner's mind worked: to show how accomplished an artist he was, he measured himself against Gaspard Dughet, a now–neglected painter whose work was highly esteemed at the time.

The usual pack of detractors pounced once again. Sir George Beaumont told Farington that *Crossing the Brook* ''appeared to him *weak* and like the work of an old man, one who no longer saw or felt colour properly; it was all of *pea-green* insipidity.'' Beaumont was the high priest of art lovers at the time, and his sallies against Turner shook their confidence in him and discouraged them from buying his work. Whatever his ulterior motives may have been, Turner varied his landscapes from one canvas to the next in an effort to give this still maligned genre the credentials and high standing it deserved.

In *Frosty Morning,* the satiny, silvery glow of daybreak envelops the silhouettes of a peasant family still numbed (ill. 54) with cold. The sky is a translucent gray, flecked with the last persistent vestiges of night. Perspective is provided by a tree stripped bare of leaves and a few stark bushes, while a shifting fog engulfs and conceals whatever lies beyond the gate to the right. All is peaceful. No bustle, no theatrics. Turner's carefully executed portrayal of countryside and humanity prefigures the humility and introspection of Millet. Little wonder that, once he had toned down his more ''sublime'' effects, Turner's work should have appealed to Mr. Fisher, the staunch patron of the arts who subsidized Constable.

Raby Castle offers a panoramic view of the countryside on an autumn morning. Here Turner developed a single (ill. 56) leitmotif, the curve, with great subtlety. The palette consists of a harmonious play of greens, golden yellows, and bluish grays. The touch is light; details are rendered with utmost care. The castle looms out of the mist, with a silvery sky overhead. The low–lying patch of haze on the left partially washes out the gently rolling hills, but this curving line is carried through in the foreground, forming a perfect oval that unobtrusively structures the entire composition. The pack of dogs strung out across the clearing and the riders scattered on the slopes have not been added simply for decorative effect; they are an indispensable part of the arrangement. The horizontal formed by the trees aligned in the middle distance acts as a focal point that is further stabilized by the bright area in the far distance. Lastly, to sustain the effect, Turner was careful to add a tangle of comparatively dark weeds in the very near foreground, thus establishing our point of view and allowing us to take in the vista in its entirety.

Turner adopted another curious, innovative, even revolutionary tack in *The Battle of Fort Rock, Val d'Aoste, Pied-* (ill. 59) *mont, 1796.* The battle scene proper is depicted in accordance with the rules governing historical subjects, but here the horror of war is underscored by the awesome natural spectacle that serves as its backdrop. The real focal point of the picture is the mountainous terrain. Our description will be as objective as possible. A huge triangle of lighter color gently wedges its tip between two other triangles that face each other, tips far apart. The lower foreground is enlivened by a few patches of vivid color. Calm prevails on the right, commotion on the left. The viewer is thrust aside, flung back; in his mind's eye he has no choice but to adopt a kind of bird's–eye view that ''pans'' the empty sweep of space before him. We feel frustrated that the vista should have to be cut off at all. Instead of simply being thrown together on the canvas, the forms mesh perfectly. The devices that Turner used for *The Battle of Fort Rock* are calculated to inspire terror, and the effect he achieved verges on the cinematographic.

A year after his return from Italy, the Royal Academy received Turner's largest canvas to date, *Rome from the* (ill. 58)

Vatican: Raffaelle Accompanied by a La Fornarina, Preparing his Pictures for the Decoration of the Loggia. This painting is both an excessive passage and an example of the mixing of genres. Given its fanciful, anachronistic mood— Bernini's celebrated colonnade had not yet been erected in Raphael's lifetime—Turner may have been indulging in a kind of "capriccio," a popular eighteenth-century device whereby a painter juxtaposed sites and monuments from diverse places and eras. As Marie-Madeleine Martinet observes, "Around 1770-1780, Willim Marlow had no qualms about surrounding St. Paul's Cathedral (London) with Venetian canals." Although Turner probably gave little time to social activity during his stint in Rome, we do know that he paid a visit to Canova and that he ran into young German and French artists who professed great admiration for Dürer and Raphael. Suddenly, the landscapes of Raphael became the darlings of the art world.

Roy Parkinson has suggested that *Rome from the Vatican* was Turner's way of marking the tricentennial of Raphael's death. John Gage, however, sees it as an autobiographical painting in which Turner wished to demonstrate his versatility: history painter, landscapist, tapestry maker, and architect (he had had a new house built at Twickenham). There is little difference between the plans Turner drew up for Sandycombe Lodge and the Palazzo Vidoni in Rome, a resemblance that smacks of megalomania. But people are generally unaware of the deeper reasons for his fascination with "the divine painter" who had been cut off in his prime. During his all-too-brief lifespan, Raphael had undertaken and completed a number of massive projects. His talent, physical appeal, his legendary love for La Fornarina—everything about him was impressive. Having showered him with honors, the Eternal City mourned him like a demigod. He was the quintessence of a handsome and beloved young man whose genius had been acknowledged by all, in other words, everything an artist like Turner—forsaken, struggling every inch of the way—longed to be.

Apparently no one understood this painting when it was exhibited, for it did not fit into any specific category. Reaction was tepid and divided; there was no buyer.

Turner exhibited sporadically at the Royal Academy until 1826, and each time his paintings were of a different genre than those he sent to the previous exhibition. However, he could take some satisfaction in seeing prominent London collectors mount exhibitions of his work. Sir John Leicester sponsored an exhibition of oils in 1819, and Walter Fawkes displayed more than sixty watercolors in 1819-1820 (2). From 1822 to 1824, his work was included in the "Splendid Drawings" exhibitions mounted by the publisher W. B. Cooke.

Because of their style, it is customary to link *The Bay of Baiae, with Apollo and the Sibyl* (R. A. 1823) and *Forum Romanum, for Mr. Soane's Museum* (R. A. 1826) to Turner's first trip to Italy.

(ill. 90)   *The Bay of Baiae* is a literary landscape that follows in the footsteps of *Crossing the Brook*. According to the legend, Apollo offered the Cumaean Sibyl the chance to live as many years as there were grains of sand in her cupped hands, but she forgot to ask for perpetual youth and grew so old that she wasted away to a shadow, only to become nothing more than a voice. Turner placed at the foot of the tree a white rabbit, symbol of Venus, and a snake, maleficent rival of mankind—both grist for commentators' mills. But *The Bay of Baiae* is remarkable above all for the subtle fluidity of its visual planes and the exquisite warmth that suffuses the landscape. Perhaps a nostalgic Turner was evoking the vanished joys of years gone by. Its soft glow alone tells of the intensity of his feelings, the poignancy of his regret.

(ill. 91)   Architectural subjects were nothing new to Turner, and *Forum Romanum* would appear to be a more fully developed venture into this branch of painting. The viewer finds himself beneath an arch that closes off the upper part of the composition and casts a gloomy shadow below. Above the majestic ruins and scattered blocks of marble we see the modern city, which fills a brighter area roughly the shape of a circle. A cleverly structured perspective at the left catches the eye, but only to lead it to some columns, while gleaming arches block the area to the right. Consequently, our interest is finally shifted to the city at the center. The juxtaposition of lighter tones is highly original. The idea for *Forum Romanum* came in large measure from what Turner saw in Italy, in addition to scattered observations of monuments elsewhere. Its asymmetry notwithstanding, this composition has a "staged" look about it. In his own way, Turner was drawing on tricks of perspective that Bibiena, Papini, and Servandoni had used in eighteenth-century theater, and which Guardi, Hubert Robert, and of course, Piranesi had popularized in painting.

Turner's trip to Italy was all but inevitable; it was a logical stop along the path of his aspirations, of his inner development. During his stay in Rome, Thomas Lawrence wrote to Farington: "Turner should come to Rome. His genius would here be supplied with materials, and entirely congenial with it...He has an elegance, and often a greatness of invention that wants a scene like this for its free expansion; whilst the subtle harmony of this atmosphere, that wraps everything in its own milky sweetness...can only be rendered, according to my belief, by the beauty of his tones" (quoted in Finberg).

52. CROSSING THE BROOK
R.A. 1815 — Oil on canvas, 193 x 165 cm
Tate Gallery, London.

53. CLAUDE LORRAIN: SEAPORT: THE EMBARKATION
OF THE QUEEN OF SHEBA
1648 — Oil on canvas, 148.6 x 193.7 cm
National Gallery, London.

54. FROSTY MORNING
R.A. 1813 — Oil on canvas, 113.5 x 174.5 cm
Tate Gallery, London.

55. DIDO BUILDING CARTHAGE, OR THE RISE OF THE
CARTHAGINIAN EMPIRE — 1st BOOK OF VIRGIL'S AENEID
R.A. 1815 — Oil on canvas, 155.5 x 233 cm
National Gallery, London.

56. RABY CASTLE, THE SEAT OF THE EARL OF DARLINGTON
R.A. 1818 — Oil on canvas, 119 x 180.6 cm
Walters Art Galley, Baltimore.

57. THE DECLINE OF THE CARTHAGINIAN EMPIRE
Rome being determined on the overthrow of her hated rival, demanded
from her such terms as might either force her into war, on ruin her by
compliance; the enervated Carthaginians, in their anxiety for peace, con-
sented to give up even their arms and their children.
R.A. 1817 — Oil on canvas. 170 x 238.5 cm

58. ROME FROM THE VATICAN. RAFFAELLE ACCOMPANIED BY LA FOR-
NARINA, PREPARING HIS PICTURES FOR THE DECORATION OF THE
LOGGIA
R.A. 1820 — Oil on canvas, 177 x 335.5 cm
Tate Gallery, London.

59. THE BATTLE OF FORT ROCK, VAL D'AOSTE, PIEDMONT, 1796
R.A. 1815 — Watercolor, 69.5 x 101 cm
British Museum, London.

60. ROME: ST. PETER'S FROM THE VILLA BARBERINI
1819 — Pencil, watercolor and gouache on white paper
prepared with a wash of grey, 22.6 x 36.8 cm
British Museum, London.

61. ROME: THE COLOSSEUM
1820 — Watercolor, 27.7 x 29.3 cm
British Museum, London.

62. ROME: THE FORUM WITH A RAINBOW
1819 — Pencil, watercolor and gouache on white paper prepared with a
wash of grey, 22.9 x 36.7 cm
British Museum, London.

63. VENICE: SAN GIORGIO MAGGIORE FROM THE DOGANA
1819 — Watercolor, 22.4 x 28.7 cm
British Museum, London.

V - DEFINITION VS. ALLUSION—
BETWEEN THE TWO TRIPS TO ITALY

The great object of life is sensation. To feel that we exist even though in pain.

Byron

No sooner do we go about the dangerous business of defining something than our minds come up with exceptions that necessitate continual readjustment and accomodation. It is an ongoing process that has no real end. However, this has not discouraged artists of every stripe from trying to structure and categorize the world by means of stable, clear–cut forms. This effort to analyze and coordinate natural phenomena through reason lies at the heart of so–called classical thought, which opts for logic and equilibrium as a way of ensuring unambiguous communication. Depending on one's point of view, it can be comforting or disheartening to realize that the classical approach can never fully achieve its goal except in science…and even there, definitions are all too often incomplete and shackled to particular moments in history.

The opposite tendency is to repudiate the powers of reason and unyielding logic in favor of imagination, sensation, and emotion. Such individuals find stability suspect and clarity repugnant; they seek refuge in relative vagueness, in a kind of quasi–unintelligibility, and attempt to communicate by means of violent, jolting forms that are better suited to surging emotions and forceful sensations. For those who subscribe to the so–called baroque view of things, reason implies mind; sensation, body.

Between these two poles—logic, precision, and explicitness on the one hand, allusion on the other—there is an infinite range of hybrid approaches. In the course of a great artist's career, his works often go through a number of phases during which one tendency or the other will gain the upper hand. Art historians, ever anxious to tie things up into neat packages, delight in reducing an oeuvre to manageable quantities, contradictions, and dominant characteristics. They calculate how much logic, how much sensation; how much imagination, how much intellect; how, when, and where order verges on disorder; how, when, and where clarity wins out over obscurity.

The thing we must bear in mind is that all of these forms come from an individual who is trying to communicate with us. They register the movement of his mind, and a mind is a dynamic, sometimes volatile phenomenon. To define and delineate is one way of getting one's bearings in the world; allusion is another. Both attitudes are articulated through cultural and historical codes; they reveal the feelings and ideologies of an era. Each is "true" in its own way, for each is a way of shaping the relationship that people try to establish between themselves and whatever it is they are looking for. They express not so much arbitrary catagories of thought as "families" of thought. In other words, beauty is, indeed, in the eye of the beholder; there is no right or wrong.

If the Enlightenment was, in theory, an admirable attempt to define and regulate natural phenomena for the benefit of mankind, it may be said that romanticism was essentially a reaction against this urge to harness and circumscribe the world. A romantic at heart, Turner lived this opposition, and for many years his classical training, artistic and social aspirations, and psychological promptings were to be continual sources of conflict. After paying a visit to Turner, the fashionable portraitist Hoppner superficially judged him "a timid man afraid to venture." But the problem went much deeper than that. Turner resisted the urgings of his body, tooth and nail. He tried to ignore the call of violent sensation, to avoid the unruliness and revolt that sensation implied. One day, however, revolt did break out, and in Turner's case the principal weapon was intense light.

As though trying to quell stirrings from within, Turner broadened the scope of his activities during this decade. Clearly, he took pride in his being named Professor of Perspective at the Royal Academy, but it was a heavy responsibility. Although his series of lectures ended in 1828, he retained his title for ten more years and often added "P.P." (Professor of Perspective) to his signature. He was, to be sure, a poor speaker and was taken to task for his lack of eloquence, but his carefully prepared drawings and diagrams made up for his infelicitous delivery.

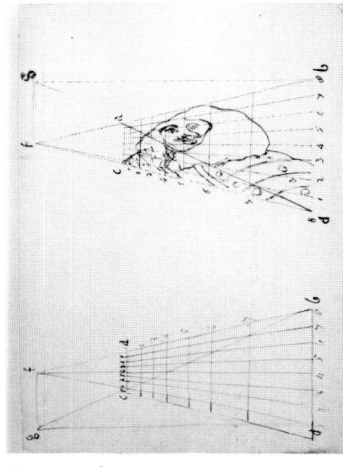

Anamorphoses

Illustration for Byron's *Poems* (1832)

As the years wore on, fewer and fewer people attended his lectures. There were times when his father, loyal to the end, was the only person in the great lecture hall of the Academy. There was something almost self–abortive about these sessions; now and again Turner would forget the date or leave his text in the carriage.

Around this time Turner illustrated the poems of Byron for a publisher named Murray and came out with a series of engravings entitled *The Rivers of England*. Before completing this series, he began work on another devoted to *Picturesque Views in England and Wales*. It took him two years to finish *Ports and Harbours of England*, for which he used the painstaking technique of line engraving. He also traveled extensively. In 1821 he journeyed to Paris by way of Dieppe, Le Havre, and Rouen; in 1824 he toured the west, northwest, and south of England; two years later he visited Brittany and traveled along the Meuse, the Moselle, and the Loire. In 1827 he spent some time with John Nash at East Cowes Castle, on the Isle of Wight, and on his return trip he stayed at Lord Egremont's estate, Petworth. The intermittent visits Turner made there over the next ten years appear to have been the few happy intervals in his life.(1)

(ill. 73) The painter was inspired by the natural beauty of the grounds at *Petworth Park: Tillington Church in the Distance*. The earl's favorite black spaniels are running to greet their master, and they form a long diagonal that heightens the impression of open, receding space. This line cuts across the elongated ellipse that emerges as the painting's key compositional element. The sun has just dipped below the horizon. Streaked with red, the sky is taking on the burnished glow of dusk. Despite the sense of calm and contentment Turner must have found at Petworth, *Petworth Park* also conveys the distressing mood of silence and loneliness that was the painter's constant companion.

That same year, Lord Egremont commissioned Turner to provide four paintings for the splendid dining room at Petworth, but they had to fit precisely into unusually proportioned spaces. Turner began work at once, and all (ill. 72, 75) four were signed in 1829. Two are of the lake at Petworth (*The Lake, Petworth: Sunset, Fighting Bucks* and *The Lake,* (ill. 70, 74) *Petworth: Sunset, A Stag Drinking*); the other two are tranquil marines (*Chichester Canal* and *Brighton Pier*). However, there seems to have been some hesitation on Turner's part. The four final versions required a total of nine preliminary oil sketches. As he progressed from studies to completed paintings, freedom and originality gave way to greater precision. Probably as a concession to Lord Egremont's conventional taste in art, Turner ended up adding a ''correct'' patina of brownish tones, but refused to sacrifice the calm, sweeping foreground, the deep perspective, the ''Turneresque'' lighting.

(ill. 82-89) Life at Petworth inspired Turner to make a series of watercolor–and–gouache sketches on grayish blue paper— wonderfully fresh, piquant sketches that glow with an exquisitely textured light. He laid on vermilions, faded pinks, lemon yellows, oranges, ochers, and unmixed whites as though his brush were bewitched. Black was treated like any other color, now blended in, now added as an accent to lighter tones. There is something marvelous in the way Turner could capture a silhouette or a mood in a flash, how he could convey a lively conversation over a cup of tea, the warmth of a bedchamber, an unmade bed unexpectedly glimpsed through a door that has been left ajar. It is not the subject that makes these watercolors so appealing, but the artist's deft, agile touch.

But Turner was no less gifted when it came to creating a more disturbing atmosphere. A feeling of mystery (ill. 87) pervades *The Sculpture Gallery*, where in the bluish semidarkness we see John Flaxman's *St. Michael Triumphant over Satan* (a subject that could not fail to impress someone like Turner). A small, hushed band of admirers are clustered about the majestic marble group; shafts of light bring into view an uncertain world in which a bat might flit by at any moment. The lack of well–defined, intelligible forms is obvious, yet the room is as unsettling as a minutely detailed picture would have been.

It may well be that Turner did not attach much importance to these on–the–spot sketches. For us, however, they provide an invaluable glimpse into how he dealt with the problem of light and color. Here the artist was free to orchestrate his palette without the Academy looking over his shoulder. The frivolous nature of his subject belies the significance of these experiments, for the colors in the Petworth sketches are anything but traditional. Turner's approach to light was based on a tonal sequence appropriate to each particular hue. Color *is* light: it delineates and creates space, it becomes ''painterly,'' that is, purely pictorial. No one knew about these little watercolors until after Turner's death, when Ruskin was finally given permission to catalogue the basketfuls of sketchbooks and papers the artist had bequeathed to the nation.

Turner's career evolved on two different levels: the paintings he exhibited at the Royal Academy or at his gallery, and those which, for various reasons, he kept hidden in his studio. Their discovery cast his work in a radically new light. The ''official'' part of his oeuvre reflects the artist as he wished to be seen: respectable, loyal to tradition, a worthy disciple of the Grand Manner. The other part includes his experiments, his bursts of defiance, his failures. Was Turner alarmed by his own freedom of invention? Did he look upon these works as a source of shame or guilt? For lack of firsthand information, we can only guess. What we cannot overlook is that this

Photograph of Petworth House, Sussex.

idiosyncratic attitude toward his work corresponded to a similar split in his private life: honored Academician on the one hand, confirmed voyeur on the other.

No one would see either *George IV at St. Giles's, Edinburgh*, and excursion into the pseudo–medieval ''Walter Scott'' manner so dear to the nineteenth century, or a marvelous oil on panel entitled *George IV at the Provost's Banquet in the Parliament House, Edinburgh*. All of the figures—the dignitaries in their gaudy red and gold attire, the king seated beneath a baldachin—seem to dissolve into the shimmering atmosphere or become blurred in the distance. Everything sparkles. Only a few spots of silvery white are needed to suggest crystal chandeliers, which are nothing more than gossamer strands of paint. The vaulted ceiling is scarcely visible, virtually impalpable, as it melts into the intense light, looking more like swirls of smoke than solid architecture. (ill. 65) (ill. 64)

Perhaps following in the footsteps of John Robert Cozens, Turner was experimenting here with a new kind of touch—a careful but unrestrained, almost casual brushwork that no longer sought to delineate objects, but to reclaim its own identity. It creates contours and movements all its own, and in so doing creates a different kind of reality: the reality of paint. The viewer no longer picks out a given object; he eventually makes out a rough equivalent of it. Vision and memory join forces, piecing together forms as his eyes jump from one blob of color to another. Variations in chromatic intensity, variations in touch, scratchings, streaks, smudges—all of this guides him along a path of discovery that can be either exhilarating or bewildering. The bedazzled Venetians, Titian in his maturity, Rembrandt *(Portarit of Jan Six)*, and Velázquez *(The Maids of Honor)* had already wrought their share of wonders with painterly brushwork. In this world of shimmering, rippling light, in this world where everything mingles and overlaps, lay the seeds of a whole current of modern painting. Light, the Impressionists discovered, was capable of altering the space it traveled across, transforming space into a magnetic field in constant, fluid motion. In an atmosphere such as this, objects with clean–cut lines would seem overdefined. Monet the painter-poet eschewed scientific rigor in favor of intuition and, at the end of his life, conceived a new way of contemplating the world.

Clearly, there was more at stake here than just another aesthetic category; an unprecedented way of looking at things was in the making. Turner must share the credit, however, with two of his contemporaries, Delacroix and Goya. Each in his own way shared in this approach to the world and depicted it with vibrant streaks and slashes of paint.

Rembrandt's Daughter (c. 1827)

With unswerving loyalty to himself, but sensitive to the way others saw him, he sent to the Royal Academy *Rembrandt's Daughter,* a variation on the love–letter theme that had been especially popular in the seventeenth century, and *Boccaccio Relating the Tale of the Birdcage.* Human figures, however numerous and detailed, always seem the neglected part of Turner's paintings. Most of them look awkward, as though rendered in what we would refer to today as a ''naive'' or ''primitive'' manner. Often they seem to be floating above the ground, and they tend to dissolve into the atmosphere, or blend in with surrounding thickets, or congeal into a tight, blurred cluster of humanity. Even though neither human beings nor animals held much interest for Turner, he included them in his paintings as a concession to convention. Landscape was the branch of art in which he felt most at home. (ill.79)

There is a famous anecdote about how a friend of Turner's added a little dog to the parapet in *Mortlake Terrace, Summer's Evening*. The artist acquiesced to the change, varnished the paper cut–out, and painted over it. It was intended to provide a focal point and has not been tampered with since, but it adds nothing to the composition. It is startlingly incongruous, and we would have no objection to seeing the dog scamper down out of sight. To our way of thinking, this black splotch mars the sweep, the boldness, the harmony of the arrangement. Be that as it may, the golden light of *Mortlake Terrace, Summer's Evening* did not appeal to critics, who thought it excessively yellow. The other painting of Mortlake Terrace, a view overlooking the Thames in the early morning, fared no better. (ill.77)

Turner made a number of sketches of the Cowes regatta before sending *East Cowes Castel, the Seat of J. Nash, Esq.: The Regatta Beating to Windward* to the Royal Academy in 1828. In one very elaborate study, a cluster of competing sailboats is buffeted by a blustering wind and the heaving swells we see in the foreground. Though executed after notes in the artist's studio, it has the freshness and vitality of firsthand experience. This power of suggestion is lacking in the version he sent to the Academy, which is circumspect, stiff, and overburdened with conventional devices. Once again the spirit of Claude had hovered over Turner as he worked out the ''correct'' blend of ingredients for the final version: proper emphasis given to the sky, the use of curved lines for their pleasantly surprising effect (recommended by Hogarth), a mood akin to that of the Dutch sea pieces that were still much appreciated by the public at large.

Mortlake Terrace

In the 1806 version of *The Battle of Trafalgar,* the artist transports the viewer into the thick of the fighting with the detailed, on–the–spot immediacy of a newspaper account. The part of the inscription that was washed off when the Thames overflowed its banks in 1928 probably gave a complete description of the circumstances surrounding (ill.66) (ill.69) the battle. In the latter part of 1823, George IV commissioned Turner to paint a scene commemorating the historic moment that marked the beginning of Napoleon's demise. It was to hang in St. James's Palace as a companion piece for an oil by Jacques–Philippe de Loutherbourg. As we examine one sketch after another, our eyes are slowly brought closer and closer to the focal point of the scene: the ship itself. The spectacle of war unfolds before us in all its chaotic horror—sinking sails still swollen by the breeze, artillery spitting fiery destruction, colors fluttering in the wind. Since that first version in 1806, Turner no longer wished to be a "war correspondent" and had come to realize that truth was not a matter of gathering eyewitness accounts and reconstructing events the way a history book would. Now he sensed that the only way to trigger emotion and inspire terror in a truly convincing manner was to excite the veiwer's imagination by means of dynamic lines, restless forms, and turbulent colors. Nothing but battered, straggling, convulsive volumes could convey the conviction of a man caught up in a lone battle with the implacable forces of destiny. By serving his country, the hero has, of his own free will, set the stage for his death. An unhappy coincidence: In May, 1824, England learned of the death of Lord Byron, who had sacrificed his life at Missolonghi to free Greece from Turkish oppression. Unfortunately, the hero had succumbed, not amid the clash of arms, but to a fever brought on by damp and cold.

East Cowes Castle, the Seat of J. Nash, Esq: The Regatta Beating to Windward (R.A. 1828)

The polished style Turner adopted for the second *Battle of Trafalgar* conveys the fury of war, to be sure, but with a restraint that showed his willingness to heed the dictates of propriety. Just the same, George IV thought the painting too unconventional, and in a humiliating blow to the artist, His Majesty ordered it removed to Greenwich Hospital in 1829.

(ill.78) Slumped over the neck of a neighing charger, the figure in *Death on a Pale Horse* is a terrifying study in black, warm browns, and steely gray. Turner scraped the paint as soon as he laid it on the canvas, as if this delicate, imperceptible, at times insubstantial layer might better convey a feeling of undefinable mystery. Here death comes into view suddenly, unexpectedly, as an embodiment of pain, as a wound incarnate. This painting, which was one of Turner's most closely guarded secrets, is clearly symbolist in spirit and cannot help bringing to mind the marvelous charcoal drawings of Odilon Redon.

Black, gray, white: Andrew Wilton believes that Turner's ongoing work with line engraving might account for the evolution of his palette during this period of his career. Indeed, there are few disciplines that can more effectively sharpen the eye and sensitize it to tonality. Every one of the countless shades of gray that lie between black and white can take on chromatic value, or at least suggest color. Turner had, it is true, the eye of a colorist, but these rigorous exercises undoubtedly had much to do with his heightened visual powers.

Turner made preparations for another trip to Italy. He had penetrated deep into the domain of vagueness and allusion. "It is not the thing itself that must be captured," wrote Delacroix, "but only a semblance of it." Would the golden light of Italy prove him correct?

Turner's elderly father died on September 21, 1829, and Finberg informs us that the painter reacted "as though he had lost an only child." Could *Death on a Pale Horse* have been, as Lawrence Gowing suggests, an expression of Turner's distress? One loss followed another: his friend Harriel Wells, the academician Dawe, and Sir Thomas Lawrence two months later (2).

(ill.67) In 1830 the Royal Academy received *The Funeral of Sir Thomas Lawrence*, a large drawing that, according to the title, Turner had sketched "from memory." It was his way of paying tribute to a man who had understood and accepted his talent for what it was. The pomp that traditionally surrounds the funerals of the famous is here conveyed by a group of figures positioned around a pool of pallid light, and by a cluster of verticals set on a base of horizontals. The harsh decree of fate is echoed in the severity of the composition.

64. GEORGE IV AT THE PROVOST'S BANQUET IN
THE PARLIAMENT HOUSE, EDINBURGH
c. 1822 — Oil on mahogany panel, 68.5 x 91.8 cm
Tate Gallery, London.

65. GEORGE IV AT ST. GILES'S, EDINBURGH
    c. 1822 — Oil on mahogany panel, 76 x 91.5 cm
    Tate Gallery, London.

66. THE BATTLE OF TRAFALGAR, AS SEEN FROM THE
    MIZEN STARBOARD SHROUDS OF THE VICTORY
    1806 — Oil on canvas, , 171 x 239 cm
    Tate Gallery, London.

67. THE FUNERAL OF SIR THOMAS LAWRENCE,
A SKETCH FROM MEMORY
R.A. 1830 — Watercolor and gouache, 61.6 x 82.5 cm
British Museum, London.

68. SECOND SKETCH FOR "THE BATTLE OF TRAFALGAR"
c. 1823 — Oil on canvas, 90 x 121 cm
Tate Gallery, London.

69. THE BATTLE OF TRAFALGAR
1823–24 — Oil on canvas, 259 x 365.8 cm
National Maritime Museum, Greenwich.

70. CHICHESTER CANAL
c. 1828 — Oil on canvas, 65.5 x 134.5 cm
Tate Gallery, London.

71. THE LAKE, PETWORTH: SUNSET
   c. 1828 — Oil on canvas, 65 x 141 cm
   Tate Gallery, London.

72. THE LAKE, PETWORTH: SUNSET, FIGHTING BUCKS
   c. 1829 — Oil on canvas, 62.2 x 146 cm Treasury and National Trust, Petworth House, Sussex.

73. PETWORTH PARK: TILLINGTON CHURCH IN THE DISTANCE
   c. 1828 — Oil on canvas, 64.5 x 145.5 cm
   Tate Gallery, London.

74. THE CHAIN PEIR, BRIGHTON
   c. 1828 — Oil on canvas, 71 x 136.5 cm
   Tate Gallery, London.

75. THE LAKE, PETWORTH: SUNSET, A STAG DRINKING
   c. 1829 — Oil on canvas, 63.5 x 132.1 cm Treasury and National Trust, Petworth House, Sussex.

76. WINDSOR CASTLE FROM SALT HILL
   c. 1806 — Oil on mahogany veneer, 27 x 73.5 cm
   Tate Gallery, London.

77. MORTLAKE TERRACE, THE SEAT OF WILLIAM MOFFATT, ESQ.
SUMMER'S EVENING
R.A. 1827 — Oil on canvas, 92 x 122 cm

78. DEATH ON A PALE HORSE
c. 1825–30 — Oil on canvas, 60 x 75.5 cm
Tate Gallery, London.

79. BOCCACCIO RELATING THE TALE OF THE BIRDCAGE
R.A. 1828 — Oil on canvas, 122 x 90.5 cm
Tate Gallery, London.

80. TWO WOMEN WITH A LETTER
c. 1835 — Oil on canvas, 122 x 91.5 cm
Tate Gallery, London.

81. PILATE WASHING HIS HANDS
R.A. 1830 — Oil on canvas, 122 x 91.5 cm
Tate Gallery, London.

ALBUM WITH SCENES AT PETWORTH
c. 1828 — Watercolors and gouaches, approx. 14 x 19 cm
British Museum, London.

82. PETWORTH: A VASE OF LILIES, DAHLIAS AND OTHER FLOWERS

84. PETWORTH: INTERIOR

83. PETWORTH: A ROOM WITH BOOKSHELVES AND A ROCOCO
    PIERGLASS, WITH SEVERAL FIGURES

85. PETWORTH: A GROUP OF WOMEN SEATED AROUND A TABLE

88. PETWORTH: A MAN SEATED AT A TABLE IN A STUDY,
EXAMINING A BOOK

86. PETWORTH: INTERIOR

89. PETWORTH: INTERIOR

87. PETWORTH: THE GALLERY, WITH FLAXMAN'S ST. MICHAEL

VI. THE IMPACT OF TURNER'S SECOND TRIP TO ITALY (AUGUST 1828–JANUARY 1829)

Illustration for Samuel Rogers's *Italy* (c. 1827)

"Light has been driven from our sight; it lies buried somewhere in our bones. It is our turn to pursue it, that its crown might be restored."

René Char

Turner went to Rome soon after handing in the last of his illustrations for Samuel Rogers's poem, *Italy*. Writing from Paris, he instructed his friend Charles Eastlake to have some canvas prepared so that he might begin work the moment he arrived. The countless sights his eyes feasted on during the second stint in Italy were to haunt his memory for many years to come. From 1830 to 1846, a year did not pass that at least one of the paintings Turner sent to the Academy did not hark back, in one way or another, to his second trip south. "he has worked here literally night and day," wrote Eastlake in a letter. "He began eight or ten pictures and exhibited three, all in about two months or a little more" (Finberg).

This urge to observe, to amass notes and sketches, might well be put down to an artist's healthy and wholly justifiable curiosity. But there were times when Turner's curiosity bordered on obsession and took on the symptoms of something more akin to anxiety. Accustomed as he was to the dreary skies of northern Europe, he could no more resist the call of Rome and Venice than his generation could break the spell of the East. Like them, he was filled with a nostalgic longing to set out in search of crimson lands far, far away.

Turner exhibited *View of Orvieto, The Vision of Medea,* and *Regulus* in Rome; *Palestrina,* which had been commissioned by Lord Egremont, was sent to the Royal Acadeny in 1830. Sixteen large sketches (never shown), and probably ten or so smaller ones, are now also believed to be direct offshoots of the second trip to Rome.

Artists and connoisseurs in both Rome and London greeted *The Vision of Medea*, in particular, with open hostility, (ill.98) while the critics stooped to downright meanness and vulgarity. At their first public showing, the canvases were mounted in painted ship's rope instead of the usual gilt frames. Although this departure from tradition was promply attributed to the painter's well-known stinginess, there may have been other reasons for this odd and innovative mode of presentation. True, he had already been taken to task for what people back then considered an outlandish, unsettling palette, but it is difficult to understand how an artist could mount pictures in so unconventional a manner without realizing that it could only further prejudice the public against his work *(Moderne Kunstchronik,* 1834). We who have lived through Cubism and Surrealism are tempted to conclude that the shock was calculated, that Turner was making a "statement."

In any event, the thing that impresses the viewer far more is how unexpected the fruits of Turner's imagination could be. The scene depicted in *The Vision of Medea* does not ring true; it smacks of an ingenuous country painter who has lost his way in the labyrinth of mythology. In spite of, perhaps because of Turner's desire to imitate Titian, there is something about its naive clumsiness that lends it a poignancy more typical of John Martin. A perceptive Eastlake noted at the time that "the figures principal [were] very bold and poetical, and most agreeable in general colour" (Finberg). However, time has faded the overall coloring to a brownish tone.

View of Orvieto (1828)

In a letter Constable wrote to James Jones, we learn that in 1829 the members of the Royal Academy intended to mount an exceptionally interesting exhibition. Most of them were planning to send at least eight paintings each. Still spurred on by the demon of competitiveness, Turner was, as usual, intent on putting together a group of works that would cause people to stand up and take notice. Among these were *Messieurs les Voyageurs on Their* (ill.100) *Return from Italy (Par la Diligence) in a Snow Drift upon Mount Tarrar—22nd of January, 1829*, a picturesque retelling in watercolor of a dramatic mishap that had befallen the painter in the dead of night; a lyrical, literary canvas entitled *The Loretto Necklace;* and the masterly *Ulysses Deriding Polyphemus—Homer's Odyssey*, a veritable panorama (ill. 96) of mythological storytelling. He had probably worked out a rough sketch of *Ulysses* while still in Rome. Since Turner admired Homer and wanted to read the *Odyssey* in the original, he agreed to give Reverend H. S. Trimmer painting lessons in exchange for what proved to be fruitless lessons in Greek. The painter settled for the celebrated translation of Alexander Pope. Rarely had so dazzling an outburst of color occurred in his work, and, not surprisingly, it was Turner's palette that raised the critics' eyebrows. ''Colouring running mad,'' the critic of *The Morning Herald* wrote, ''positive vermilion, positive indigo, and all the most glaring tints of green, yellow and purple.''

Atop an awesome mountain promontory we see the Cyclops, contorted in agony as evening mists gather. A series of arched rock formations closes the bay in which the fleet had taken refuge a while before. The ships are hurriedly preparing to weigh anchor. Beams radiating from the still glistening sun fan out across the majestic sweep of sky and transform the sea into a vast, golden reflection. Alternating warm and cool tones crate a play of dazzling light and colored shade that bewilders the eyes.

In a flourish of eruditon and poetic conceit, Turner transformed the foamy waves at the ship's prow into silvery Nereids, their foreheads bedecked with stars, and borrowed the sun's chariot from the east pediment of the Parthenon. The latter allusion to Greek mythology was probably a last minute addition and, therefore, not blended in very well with the pigments; overzealous cleaning has all but obliterated it. The moment the artist decided to capture is highly dramatic: from his ship, Ulysses is hurling abuse at the terrifying, but now vanquished monster. Everything conspires to give *Ulysses Deriding Polyphemus* the sublime, heroic tone that tradition called for. As Ruskin points out, ''*Polyphemus* asserts his perfect power and is, therefore, to be considered as the *central picture* in Turner's career.'' Above all, however, *Ulysses* is a pivotal work because, more than any other painting, it was the first to reveal fully Turner's preoccupation with light, the ''luminism'' that was to become the hallmark of his oeuvre.

One of the more idiosyncratic facets of Turner's sensibility was that he always proceeded in an erratic, at times contradictory manner. Works signed in the space of a single year show marked differences in style and genre. A consummate artist merely attempting to demonstrate just how broad a spectrum his virtuosity covered? Or was this diversity symptomatic of a deeper instability that made it impossible for him to confine his quest to a single manner or approach?

(ill.81)   Suddenly, Turner produced a series of curious paintings that seem to have been inspired by Rembrandt: *Pilate*
(ill.117)   *Washing His Hands* (with a quote from Matthew); *Jessica*, a subject that carried with it the unassailable prestige of Shakespeare; and *Shadrach, Meshach and Abednego in the Burning Fiery Furnace*, with a quote from the Book of Daniel. Indeed, a number of elements are reminiscent of Rembrandt's style: the inner glow that seems to radiate from deep within the paint itself; the dense, ill–defined crowds that Turner returned to time and again; the frontal treatment of a strange, bejewelled Jessica, captured as she is about to close the window in accordance with Shylock's command.

(ill.115)   The *Study of Watteau* was intended to provide a theoretical and technical illustration of a rule in Fresnoy's *L'Art de peindre*: ''When white shines forth clear and pure, it can make an object seem either closer or farther away.'' At the same time, a scheming, perhaps spiteful Turner had availed himself of an opportunity to show all those who had criticized his palette for its unorthodoxy or excessive brilliance how subtle his eye, and how austere his pictorial aims, could be.

(ill.93,95)   In *Caligula's Palace and Bridge* and *Childe Harold's Pilgrimage*, Turner once again sounded the leitmotifs that crop up time and again in his work. To sing the glories of Italy, he turned to Byron and the fervor that the poet concealed beneath a facade of violence and provocation; to bemoan faded glory, dethroned rulers, and crumbled kingdoms, he used an excerpt from his own unfinished poem, *The Fallacies of Hope*. Two massive, majestic canvases in which the painter bares his soul and reveals, now his romantic love for vastness, now his distress and grief in the face of all that is fallen, shattered, ruined. Even a veneer of mellowness cannot mask the underlying sense of fear or dread that threatens to break through the surface at any moment. Downfall signifies the triumph of time over man, and there is always something about immensity, about boundless sweeps of space, that prompts man to take stock of his paltriness.

At a certain point in his career, Turner began to re–examine and re–evaluate what had been until then an unquestioning respect for approved hierarchies and an intense admiration for that bulwark of the Grand Manner, ''high'' or ''elevated'' art. His compositions became more relaxed, the asymmetry that had already distinguished his style from that of Claude, more fluid. True, the ''egg'' or ''womb,'' call it what you will, around which he never tired of structuring his works grew less conspicuous, but it is there neverthelss. Apparently the artist still looked to this profoundly fascinating oval shape as a kind of refuge. ''The outsider finds himself drawn inside,'' observes Gaston Bachelard. ''We cannot overemphasize the importance of these framed dreams in which the act of contemplation is accomplished by a hidden contemplator. If there is grandeur in the scene, the person musing on it semms to experience a rhythmic oscillation between immensity and intimacy, a dialectical state that affords him now effusiveness, now security.'' Security...Can we not trace it all the way back to ''the more tranquil existence before birth''? The restlessness that characterized Turner's entire life may have been a manifestation of conflicting desires on an unconscious level.

The reviews of *Caligula's Palace and Bridge* were highly favorable, and the *Times* hailed it.

Illustration for Samuel
Rogers's *Italy* (c. 1827)

Illustration for Byron's *Poems*
(1832)

In 1831, an unenthusiastic Turner agreed to illustrate the poems of Sir Walter Scott. It has been said that his sole reason for taking on the job was the handsome fee it commanded. To quote Walter Scott. ''Turner's palm is as itchy as his hands are ingenious, and he will, take my word for it, do nothing without cash and anything for it.'' Turner had hoped to save the cost of a trip to Scotland by drawing on the reserve of sketches and drawings he had amassed during his last journey north, but Scott himself and Robert Cadell, who was publishing his collected works, insisted that the painter visit certain sites mentioned in the poems. It was no mean undertaking, one that was expanded to include all of Scott's prose works. The complete edition comprised forty volumes, which were brought out over a four–year period (1832-1836).

Turner set out for Scotland in August, 1831. First he spent some time at Abbotsford Castle, where he found Walter Scott toiling like a convict to pay off his debts, then proceeded across the country. On his return trip, he made an excursion by boat to the islands of Staffa and Iona on the west coast. What destination could be more romantic, more appealing than Fingal's Cave? Only two years earlier, a deeply impressed Mendelssohn had come away from his visit to the cave with a rough draft of his symphonic poem; Turner, for his part, painted *Staffa,* (ill. 107) *Fingal's Cave.* He described the experience in a letter to James Lenox. ''The sun getting toward the horizon, burst through the raincloud, angry and for wind; and so it proved, for we were driven from shelter into Loch Ulver.'' The elements Turner brings together in this tense, gloomy painting conjure up an atmosphere that is heavy with foreboding. Night is falling. The red sun is ebout to dip below the horizon, and gusts of wind are whipping the sea into mighty swells. With the towering cliff as a backdrop, a ship is battling the storm, straining to avoid being driven against the fog–shrouded rocks.

Everything is at once romantic and realistic, and therein lies the dilemma. Turner decided to paint, not some old, graceful schooner with tattered sails, but a steamship belching a column of black, acrid smoke—a banal, monstrous piece of flotsam tossed up by the wave of industrialization that began sweeping over England in the early eighteenth century. In this case, he did not find it necessary to invoke the Muse. What is it, then, that gives this scene its romantic flavor? Everything about *Staffa, Fingal's Cave*—line, form, color—helps convey a *mood*. At the time of the excursion, Turner's heart really was in his mouth, and painting was his way of expressing his terror at the unbridled forces of nature. Equally romantic is the way he positioned and exaggerated certain compositional elements—the crest of the cliff (which is repeated and extended a bit lower by the thick smoke), the long, low horizontal of the sea, the majestic sweep of brightness—as is the intense, turbulent brushwork. Turner's aim was not so much to ''report'' what he had seen as to do everything in his power to impress the viewer and convey his excitement. Where is the dividing line?

Whereas *The Golden Bough* follows in the tradition of *Childe Harold's Pilgrimage* and even the earlier *Bay of Baiae* in (ill. 94, 95, 90) that it evokes a poetic, mythological Greece suffused in an elegaic light, *Keelmen Heaving in Coals by Moonlight* and *The Burning of the Houses of Lords and Commons, 16th of October 1834* are both eyewitness accounts of events from everyday life and thus open up the possibility of historical implications.

It has been said that Turner was sensible and level–headed where politics were concerned, which means that, in those troubled times, he respected established authority regardless of who might have been at the helm. Generally speaking, he probably favored the steady flow of continuity. Apparently he was not one of those who, at a certain moment in history, saw in Napoleon Bonaparte the liberating hero of the modern age. Moreover, his clients came from the up–and–coming middle class, the new founders and captains of industry, as well as from the aristocracy.

Just the same, the shift of the most destitute strata of society to major urban centers was having tragic consequences. Unbearable working conditions—when there was work—sowed the seeds of rebellion; rebellion bred repression. Workers had to adapt themselves to industrial production, and a growing sense of malaise began to creep over the landscape. Some, like Charles Dickens, felt that appalling poverty was turning the cities into dens of vice and human degradation. Man lived lost in the crowd, yet utterly alone.

Although Dickens was getting ready to denounce openly the frightful wretchedness that was rampant in England at the time, he did not feel beholden to propose another type of society. He was moved, to be sure, but more to tears than to action. It was left to the social theorists of the nineteenth century to come up with alternatives.

There is nothing in Turner's work to indicate where he stood on these issues. His peasants are humble and patient; his hero–fishermen struggle valiantly with the wild sea; his coal-heavers and stevedores conscientiously apply themselves to their tasks. At least, that is how the latter are portrayed in a painting commissioned by Henry McConnell, *Keelmen Heaving in Coals by Moonlight.* (A rough draft of this canvas had already been worked (ill. 109) out back in 1823 as *Shields on the River Tyne,* a watercolor from the *Rivers of England* and *Ports and Harbours of England* series.) Long streaks of blue extend across a yellowish sky that is mirrored in the calm, shimmering waters of the Tyne. The reddish glow of firelight enlivens and helps to separate the tangled cluster of moored ships. Two dark spots, a buoy and a rat, have been carefully positioned in the foreground to heighten the sense of depth created by the great, tunnellike swirl of smoke. *Keelmen Heaving in Coals by Moonlight* confronted the painter with the problem of structuring a chiaroscuro study around several light sources of different intensity and brightness. Not only did he solve it admirably and with uncommon subtlety, but also managed to convey the grayish eerieness that prevails just before daybreak.

As soon as the news reached him, Turner rushed to the banks of the Thames to witness the conflagration that had engulfed the Houses of Parliament. His appetite for catastrophe having been whetted, he sketched the scene (ill. 105) feverishly and followed up with two paintings of the fire (exhibited the same year) and a nearly finished watercolor.

(ill. 106) With its palette of red, green, yellow, blue, and red, this dazzling canvas looks, if anything, more like a celebration than a tragic event (even if, as has been suggested, it has political overtones). The ghostly bridge, festooned with lanterns and severed in two by the glow of the fire, the hurried, scraped brushstrokes of the boats on the Thames—everything creates an atmosphere that is more in keeping with a festive regatta. In the distance, the colored rockets of a lavish fireworks display are showering windswept, incandescent sparks on a crowd that is more dumbfounded than terror-stricken. One would think that William Beckford, the richest man in England, were treating the Who's Who of London to a summertime Venetian carnival along the banks of the Thames. Actually, the glittering conflagration provided Turner with a logical (and long-awaited) opportunity to show the public just how bold vagueness could be, how unbridled and impassioned an artistic vision could be. That is, unless, as Andrew Wilton has suggested, one sees in his work "...a symbolic record of the destruction by reform of the old, corrupt Parliamentary system."

For all its sugary sentimentality, eighteenth-century England had secreted the horrors of the slave trade like pus oozing from a wound (although we should bear in mind that it was the first society to clear its conscience by abolishing it in 1833). Terrible accounts were circulating at the time about the activities of these cruel, greedy, cynical merchants, in particular, about the captain of the slavetrader *Zong,* who ordered his "cargo" thrown overboard so that he could say they were lost at sea and claim insurance. (Slaves who fell ill or died on board were not insured.) Though somewhat belatedly, Turner painted an impressive, uncanny oil whose title leads us to (ill. 108) believe that he was speaking out against the atrocious traffic in human life: *Slavers Throwing Overboard the Dead and Dying—Typhon Coming On (The Slave Ship).*

Beneath a red and yellow sky flecked with pale glimmers of light and slashed from top to bottom by a "fiery path" (Ruskin), a ship maneuvering through a squall has left in its wake a flotsam of debris and human limbs. A cruel cluster of birds and monstrous fish has already begun to descend. Thwarting all logical expectations, heavy shackles float on the waves like so many instruments out of some erotic fantasy, while in the foreground a woman's still-fettered leg—how delicately arched the foot is!—emerges from a rustling, frothy petticoat of fish lured by the meal. "Thus, a twofold awareness emerges, an awareness that unites, on the one hand, a specific visual image that is the subject of lengthy commentary and, on the other hand, a image of undefinable, emotionally-charged intimacy" (Gaston Bachelard). As we ponder the hidden meaning of the many details the artist so lovingly brought together in this single painting, the following question arises: Did he share the victims' suffering, or did he derive from this scene a morally repugnant sense of self-satisfaction? The verses appended to the title have a curious ring to them:

> "...the dead and dying—ne'er heed
> their chains.
> Hope, Hope, fallacious Hope!
> Where is they market now?"

In his sublime description of *The Slave Ship* in *Modern Painters,* an impassioned Ruskin says nothing about the subject, concentrating instead on the stormy landscape.

Traditionally, critics have, to varying degrees, linked form and content. Today, however, they are no longer regarded as inescapable, consubstantial elements of a dialectic. With good reason, we tend to give priority to structures and how they interact, regardless of the artist's emotions, or the events of his life at the time, or the ostensible subject of the work under discussion. As a result, territory that has already been explored and charted is turning up new information and insights. Art is becoming increasingly autonomous; it is revealing more of its own world even as it reflects the one around us, that play of fragmented mirror images we think we know so well. As the field of inquiry into the mystery of creation broadens, we are catching glimpses of vistas we never thought existed.

90. THE BAY OF BAIAE, WITH APOLLO AND THE SIBYL
   R.A. 1823 — Oil on canvas, 145.5 x 239 cm
   Tate Gallery, London.

91. FORUM ROMANUM, FOR MR. SOANE'S MUSEUM
   R.A. 1826 — Oil on canvas, 145.4 x 237.5 cm
   Tate Gallery, London.

92. PALESTRINA — COMPOSITION
   1828–30 — Oil on canvas, 140.5 X 249 cm
   Tate Gallery, London.

93. CALIGULA'S PALACE AND BRIDGE
R.A. 1831 — Oil on canvas, 137 x 246.5 cm
Tate Gallery, London.

94. THE GOLDEN BOUGH
R.A. 1834 — Oil on canvas, 104 x 163.5 cm
Tate Gallery, London.

95. CHILDE HAROLD'S PILGRIMAGE — ITALY
R.A. 1832 — Oil on canvas, 142 x 248 cm
Tate Gallery, London.

96. ULYSSES DERIDING POLYPHEMUS — HOMER'S ODYSSEY
   R.A. 1829 — Oil on canvas, 132.5 x 203 cm
   National Gallery, London.

97. REGULUS
1828–29 — Oil on canvas, 91 x 124 cm

98. THE VISION OF MEDEA
1828 — Oil on canvas, 173.5 x 241 cm
Tate Gallery, London.

99. THE PARTING OF HERO AND LEANDER — FROM
THE GREEK OF MUSAEUS
R.A. 1837 — Oil on canvas, 146 x 236 cm
National Gallery, London.

100. MESSIEURS LES VOYAGEURS ON THEIR RETURN
FROM ITALY (PAR LA DILIGENCE) IN A SNOW DRIFT
UPON MOUNT TARRAR — 22ND OF JANUARY, 1829
R.A. 1829 — Watercolor and gouache, 54 x 74 cm
British Museum, London.

101. PAESTUM IN A THUNDERSTORM
c. 1825 — Watercolor with pencil, 21.3 x 30.5 cm
British Museum, London.

102. RICHMOND HILL AND BRIDGE, SURREY
c. 1831 — Watercolor and some gouache, 29.1 x 43.5 cm
British Museum, London.

103. HOLY ISLAND, NORTHUMBERLAND
c. 1829 — Watercolor, with some gouache and scraping-out,
pen and black ink, 29.2 x 43.2 cm
Victoria and Albert Museum, London.

104. LOUTH, LINCOLNSHIRE
c. 1827 — Watercolor and scraping-out, 28.5 x 42 cm
British Museum, London.

105. THE BURNING OF THE HOUSES OF PARLIAMENT
1834 — Watercolor and gouache, 29.3 x 44 cm
British Museum, London.

106. THE BURNING OF THE HOUSES OF LORDS
AND COMMONS, 16TH OF OCTOBER 1834
1835 — Oil on canvas, 91.5 x 123 cm
Philadelphia Museum of Art, John H. McFadden Collection

107. STAFFA, FINGAL'S CAVE
R.A. 1832 — Oil on canvas, 91.5 x 122 cm
Yale Center for British Art, Paul Mellon Collection.

108. SLAVERS THROWING OVERBOARD THE DEAD AND
DYING — TYPHON COMING ON (THE SLAVE SHIP)
R.A. 1840 — Oil on canvas, 91 x 138 cm
Museum of Fine Arts, Boston.

109. KEELMEN HEAVING IN COALS BY MOONLIGHT
R.A. 1835 — Oil on canvas, 90.2 x 121.9 cm
National Gallery of Art, Washington, D.C.

VII. ISOLATION (I): 1836–1846

"Light is like water: It makes its way willy-nilly and finds its level instantaneously."   *Ingres*

As far as traditionalists were concerned, *The Parting of Hero and Leander—From the Greek of Musaeus* was, in terms of (ill. 99)
style, one of Turner's last "tolerable" paintings. According to Hamerton and even Finberg—the latter's *Life of
J. M. W. Turner, R. A.* has been called "as conservative as it is useful"—everything that came after was the product
of an artist that had succumbed to senility. What other logical explanation could there be for the "baffling" works
of Turner's late period?...

The heap of buildings, the way the group in the foreground counterbalances the turbulent skies overhead and
the tangled cluster of sea gods to the right—all this people could still accept. Although this fanciful scene appealed to Francis Danby, William Etty, and other young artists whose enthusiasm may have been fueled by a
certain need to compete with the art establishment, it also triggered less positive, but equally spirited reactions
from a number of critics. It was Rev. John Eagles's scathing attacks in *Blackwood's Magazine* that prompted Ruskin
to take up Turner's cause. These jibes touched a raw nerve in the artist, and there are several anecdotes to confirm
how deeply distressed he was by them. As Sara Coleridge wrote, "The public thought Turner was laughing at
them, and they laughed at him." Their criticism mortified his complex and, at times, paradoxically scheming
sincerity, not to mention his deep and total commitment to his work.

It is likely that these bitter disappointments, coupled with hypochondria, illness (1845), and the loss of close
friends, accentuated the painter's tendency to aloofness and solitude. A letter Disraeli wrote to Lady Bradford in
1875 implies that his vision may have also been a source of concern at the time (1).

The precision so dear to Dutch painters is conspicuous in the monumental marine, *The Prince of Orange, William* (ill. 111)
III, Embarked from Holland, Landed at Torbay, November 4th, 1688, after a Stormy Passage; but in *The 'Fighting Téméraire'* (ill. 110)
Tugged to Her Last Berth to Be Broken Up (1838), Turner worked out a delicate balance of blurred and sharply defined
forms. Indeed, it is this subtle play of precision and allusion that conveys the painter's feelings, in this case, his
dejection. The historic vessel had won fame at the battle of Trafalgar when she attempted to cover Nelson's ship.
When the admiral told her to keep back, she obeyed and remained unperturbed as she came under enemy fire.
The *Téméraire* was, and still is, a symbol of naval heroism and has moved countless Englishmen to tears. Like
some gallant old warrior grown too decrepit to be of any useful service, the disabled ship is being towed to drydock by a "little demon of a steamer" (Ruskin) to be broken up. Silhouetted against a wan, greyish-blue sky
scarred by long streaks of yellow and ocher red, the ghostly *Téméraire*, all of her sails taken in, glides forward to the
muted, rhythmic accompaniment of the little tugboat with its belching smokestack. The lack of grandiloquence
makes the feeling of solitude that much more poignant. Louis Hawes believed that Turner was musing on his
own declining years and death as he painted this picture, with Turner himself, or artists in general, cast in the role
of hero. In any event, *'Fighting Téméraire'* is an example of how creativity knows no timetable, for it was based on a
cheerful sketch Turner had drawn in 1832: a picturesque juxtaposition of the old and the new—sail power and
steam power—along the banks of the Seine.

Historians seem to agree that a similar meaning is to be found in two other works, *War. The Exile and the Rock Limpet* (ill. 112)
and its pendant, *Peace—Burial at Sea.* Contrary to what Ruskin said, the thing we find most absorbing about the (ill. 113)
latter is the uncanny beauty of those solemn, black sails that are as cold as death itself. They are an intense,
forlorn black that confirms the depth of the painter's anguish. His reply to a disapproving votary of verisimilitude
was, "I only wish I had any colour to make them blacker." They give rise to a series of associations in the viewer's
mind. The hard-edged sails make one feel as though one were standing at the edge of a cave or tomb, gloomy
apertures which, according to Gaston Bachelard, play a significant role in man's unconscious. "How can this
simple black hole serve as a valid image of deep inner vision? There must be an abundance of earthly reverie, a

musing on deep, intangible black, a black whose only tangible reality is its depth.'' The black ship, its black stiff sails that stand out against the fiery glow of an impossible mortuary chapel, give ''the impression that, within this same realm of depth, cavernous lights are answering the painter's gaze with a searching gaze of their own.'' Turner's ostensible purpose may have been to ''report'' an event or spectacle on canvas, but his use of color tells us that he was not aiming at description in the ordinary sense of the word. By now he had learned to build form through color, form which, though still stable, often seems on the verge of disintegration. Now every picture he painted had an intrinsic ''truth'' all its own.

Lord Egremont, the friend to whom Turner owed perhaps the most carefree (at any rate, least anguished) moments of his life, died in 1837. Between 1835 and 1837, the artist painted a series of unexhibited pictures that recall (ill.118,114) the peaceful hours he spent in this aristocratic setting: *Music Party, Petworth, Interior at Petworth, A Vaulted Hall,* and others. Probably these works were done from memory, for they do not ''depict'' so much as they evoke or suggest. As the viewer contemplates them, he finds himself drenched in an intense, glaring light that is as bewildering as total darkness. Like a torrent that has suddenly been released, it surges beneath arches and overwhelms everything in its path. This red and yellow sea of primordial, elemental light swallows up interiors and musicians alike, transforming them into a world without substance. Actually, these works encompass a broad range of light, for he let his imagination guide his choice of chromatic key. The only recurrent motif is the arch, a variant of the highly symbolic vault; it appears in one painting after another almost to the point of obsession. In a masterly reversal, Turner takes us into what looks like an underground domain where everything is nebulous and uncertain.

Perplexed art historians note that these parlors, corridors, and waiting rooms are nowhere to be found at the real Petworth. The odd catafalque with a coat of arms in *Interior at Petworth* remains a mystery. Some point out that the architect Soane celebrated his purchase of an Egyptian sarcophagus by holding a three–day reception and that Turner, who was one of the guests, may have made a mental note of the sarcophagus and pieced together a rough equivalent later on. However, the catafalque we see here brings to mind the gilded splendor of a funeral in Venice, not the boat the Egyptians believed ferried the souls of the dead.

Turner's tour of the continent in 1833, which brought him to Paris, Berlin, Dresden, Prague, and Vienna, probably also included a stint in Venice. He began the ''Petworth'' paintings two years later, and the one most reminiscent of Venice, *Interior at Petworth,* dates from 1837. How could this brooding soul given to melancholy and dejection not be moved by this city—now forlorn, now suddenly whimsical—a city that was being eaten away by sea salt and slowly sinking into the pale, yellowish–green waters of the lagoon? As he strolled through Venice, he may well have observed or caught glimpses of the same majestic archways, the same spacious, vaulted rooms, the same dim corridors that would suddenly open onto deserted drawing rooms, their walls covered with faded frescos and tarnished mirrors, inhabited only by boisterous dogs and cackling hens. Though (ill. 131) rendered in medium of different intensity and consistency, the watercolor entitled *Room in Venice* is quite close in spirit to *Interior at Petworth.* With its opalescent light and white ceilings festooned with a flurry of garlands, this space snares the viewer into a state of repose. The room dissolves, disintegrates into a play of red and blue and the lemon yellow of the mosquito netting. The drapes have been left open to sway in a soothing, maternal sea breeze. Venice babbles in the distance.

(ill. 119-124) Turner became obsessed with Venice toward the end of his life. According to Andrew Wilton's catalogue, between 1833 and 1845 Turner exhibited no fewer than twenty Venetian subjects at the Royal Academy and kept eight others secret. If we limit ourselves to finished, if not as yet precisely dated works, his last trip to Venice in (ill.125-131) 1840, at age sixty–five, yielded twenty–four watercolors and a vast amount of studies and sketches drawn both in bound sketchbooks and on loose leafs.

He ogled the city like a voyeur, scrutinizing and setting down her many charms: her silky gown of water, her iridescent dawns, the shifting, moiréd oranges, greens, reds, and mauves of her sunsets, her gentleness and tranquility in bright weather, the havoc she endured in storms. He peered into her, delved into the ripples and eddies left by gondolas gliding on the serene lagoon. Flashes of lightning illuminate the Piazzetta, while the Doge's Palace, San Giorgio Maggiore, and Santa Maria Della Salute loom in the pink and azure mists of daybreak.

(ill. 122) Oils were a more natural medium for her rituals, solemn ceremonies, celebrations, and processions. In *Venice: The Piazzetta with the Ceremony of the Doge Marrying the Sea,* the pearly city fades into the light of an indolent, tepid afternoon. At the edge of the *palazzi* we see the swirling, coiling reflections of a Venice bedecked in crimson velvet. The one thing that Turner's oils and watercolors of Venice have in common is light—light in all its shuddering diversity, its silky whiteness. It is an ecstatic, sparkling light as dazzling as a silvery blade glistening in the moonlight. In Turner's pictures, ''light is not only glorious and sacred, it is voracious, carnivorous, unsparing. It devours impartially, without distinction, the whole living world'' (Lawrence Gowing).

In 1836, the manic light that surges though Turner's Venetian pictures once again gave the irascible Rev. John Eagles a chance to vent his spleen. As a disciple of logic and verisimilitude, he could find nothing in them but

A Vaulted Hall (c. 1835)

"absurdities." Ruskin, who was all of eighteen at the time, waxed indignant and prepared a fiery rebuttal. Turner, however, thought it best to lick his wounds in silence. But an infuriated Ruskin came up with the idea of writing *Modern Painters* in order to vindicate Turner and help his contemporaries see how they had been blinded by prejudice.

It might appear that some critics have made far too much of Turner's pessimism, an allegation that certainly could be leveled at Jack Lindsay, but also at all those who detect in Turner's paintings the symptoms of a frustration ready to break through the surface at any moment. Of course, everything is ambivalent, and Turner the pessimist must have had his share of happy moments. However, pessimism can assume any number of guises; its metaphors are many. It is, to be sure, a mediocre patchwork of a poem, but *The Fallacies of Hope* still proclaims Turner's disappointment and the futility of optimism. If the light of Venice, for all its unforeseen bursts of glee, must be so intense, so glaring, perhaps it is because the slightest touch threatened to irritate the sore. For Turner, light concealed the wound.

Venice: The Dogana and San Giorgio Maggiore (R.A. 1834)

Darkness suits the sublime in the same manner that mourning becomes Electra. In Turner's work, light and darkness are two sides of the same coin, and the artist immersed himself now in one, now the other. They are not contradictory phenomena, a conclusion one may be tempted to draw from two paintings Turner exhibited simultaneously at the Royal Academy in 1843: *Shade and Darkness—The Evening of the Deluge* and *Light and Colour (Goethe's Theory)—The Morning after the Deluge—Moses Writing the Book of Genesis.* Both were related to Turner's reading of Goethe's recently translated *Farbenlehre,* or *Theory of Colors,* a spiritualistic theory that was at variance with Newton's analysis of the spectrum. Judging by comments written in the margin of his copy, Turner seems to have been especially struck by the chapter entitled "Physical–Psychic Effect of Color." "It has been amply demonstrated that a color makes a particular impression on human beings and, in so doing, reveals its essence to the eyes and feelings together" (#915). Before ending his discussion, Goethe observes that "if our *Theory of Colors* should meet with the reader's approval, it cannot help leading to allegorical, symbolic, and mystical applications and interpretations, depending on the spirit of the times" (#920). (ill. 134, 133)

In *Shade and Darkness,* an ellipse of pallid light brings into view a gloomy, inchoate magma of muted, overlapping reds and yellows. We can just make out a few scattered human figures and some animals that are chained or busy grazing. A group of birds on the wing, forming another arc, is about to plunge into the warm cavernous womb of light. Bold, slashing brushwork causes the paint to wriggle and gesticulate before our eyes. The viewer has no recourse but to be swallowed up by the light as he makes his way along a peninsula in the distance and out toward a sea beset by undiscernible convulsions. Here again is the vortex that man, lost and forever bewildered, longs to rediscover; here again is a tragic painting that brings the hidden obsessions of its creator to the fore.

Goethe based his theory of colors on a chromatic circle and assigned each of them a "plus" or "minus" value. Warm tones—yellows, reddish–yellows (oranges), and yellowish reds—were all plus colors associated with "vivacity." Greens, blues, and violets (the so–called cold tones) were considered "minuses" and identified with dejection. Except for a small patch of blue in the upper right–hand corner of the canvas, *Light and Colour* is structured around a blend of reds and yellows, the latter being, as Goethe put it, "the color nearest to light." Human beings adrift in an otherworldly ether are being swept along in yet another whirlwind, swirling about the figure of Moses that looms out of the clouds. What looks like a red and bluish promontory emerges from deep within the light; the staff driven into it—the emblem of the leader, the father, as well as a phallic symbol that suggests fire and shooting sparks—has been transformed into the Brazen Serpent.

In 1846, Turner sent to the Royal Academy *Undine Giving the Ring to Masaniello, Fisherman of Naples* and *The Angel Standing in the Sun.* The main compositional element in both paintings is the circle. The viewer is led to what looks like the orifice of a dark, narrow passageway that suddenly opens onto a spinning, luminous fairyland of colors. In *Undine,* a variation on the ring theme, there are actually two circles of light. This circle–within–a–circle structure focuses our attention not only on the ring image proper, but on the underlying message of power it conveys (and which Ruskin had begun to fathom). The Chinese believed that certain jade rings (*pi*) could communicate with Heaven, but as far as Western civilization is concerned, rings symbolize, among other things, a pledge and a common destiny. To this day, we consider the ring a token of fidelity. In addition, Turner may have been familiar with various Irish legends that ascribe to rings the power of self–recognition or self–identification. Was not Turner driven by a search for identity and recognition, a yearning to belong to the holy alliance of honored Academicians? (ill. 135, 136)

The central figure in *The Angel Standing in the Sun* is lifting his sword over a mottled world thronged with scarcely identifiable forms that seem to be either crawling about fitfully or striking poses of prostration and despair. Some have suggested a possible allusion to Judith or Delilah. Be that as it may, the beings in both this painting and *Undine* move about within a cramped space that is moist, flowing, warm; they are half-hidden by swirling, phosphorescent mists that seem to rise from the shuddering bowels of the earth. The image would not be complete without an area of shimmering water. "All things considered, confined space is a kind of primordial (ill. 136) impression," observes Gaston Bachelard. "As we probe our memories, we rediscover a far-off land where space is nothing more than a path. Only this pathway of space, this arduous pathway of space allows the mighty, dynamic dreams that we relive with our eyes closed, in that deepest slumber where we rediscover our unseen life in all its intimacy." The symbolic images that recur in these paintings once again bring us back to the maternal presence/absence that loomed so large in Turner's life, both physically and emotionally, back to the void that his beloved Royal Academy may have helped to fill.

Yet, even Turner's "luminous" paintings are overshadowed by a sense of gloom that would creep in as he made the transition from literary concept to pictorial equivalent. As Ruskin put it, "There never was yet, so far as I can hear or read, isolation of a great spirit so utterly desolate...My own admiration of him was wild in enthusiasm, but it gave him no ray of pleasure; he could not make me at that time understand his main meanings, he loved me, but cared nothing for what I said." How saddening it is to read this and recall that Ruskin was Turner's unwavering admirer and staunchest defender! Is not uncommunicativeness a symptom of irreversible withdrawal and solitude? Is it not the breeding ground of fantasy?

Until recently, most of Turner's biographers, beginning with Ruskin, have rebelled against Thornbury's insinuations. A. J. Finberg, for example, was so anxious to keep Turner's Victorian respectability intact that he indulged in outright angelism. As though spellbound with admiration, critics were once inclined to idealize things and felt compelled to lift so-called geniuses above the level of lowly mortals. Nowadays, we have come to regard the kind of bitter, sublimated inner turmoil Turner endured as something that can impel an individual to create. "Genius is an alchemy," observed the great Portugese poet Fernando Pessoa. "The alchemical process consists of four stages: 1)decomposition; 2)calcination; 3)rubefaction; 4)sublimation. After sensations have been allowed to decay, they are calcinated in one's memory, then rubefied by means of the imagination, and finally expressed in a sublimated form."

Sublimation through expression—that is what Ruskin failed to understand when he decided that a large parcel of erotic drawings he had come across while cataloguing the Turner Bequest should be burned. "And while he lived in imagination in ancient Carthage, lived, practically, in modern Margate. I cannot understand these ways of his." And because he could not understand, he interfered; today we rightly condemn what he did as unconscionable. Granted, Ruskin's unorthodox education did not make it easy for him to accord Turner's work the comprehension and respect it deserved, the work of a tortured man who tried to break a vicious cycle of pain and dejection by watching and sketching erotic scenes.

Ruskin's letter to Wornum, which Andrew Wilton discovered in the National Gallery Library, is proof positive that these drawings existed and that they were, in fact, destroyed (2).

110. THE 'FIGHTING TEMERAIRE' TUGGED TO HER
LAST BERTH TO BE BROKEN UP, 1838
R.A. 1839 — Oil on canvas, 91 x 122 cm
National Gallery, London.

111. PRINCE OF ORANGE, WILLIAM III, EMBARKED FROM HOLLAND,
LANDED AT TORBAY, NOVEMBER 4TH, 1688, AFTER A STORMY
PASSAGE
R.A. 1832 — Oil on canvas, 90.5 x 120 cm
Tate Gallery, London.

112. WAR, THE EXILE AND THE ROCK LIMPET
R.A. 1842 — Oil on canvas, 79.5 x 79.5 cm
Tate Gallery, London.

113. PEACE—BURIAL AT SEA
R.A. 1842 — Oil on canvas, 87 x 86.5 cm
Tate Gallery, London.

114. INTERIOR AT PETWORTH
c. 1837 — Oil on canvas, 91 x 122 cm
Tate Gallery, London.

115. STUDY OF WATTEAU BASED ON FRESNOY'S RULES
R.A. 1831 — Oil on oak panel, 40.5 x 70 cm
Tate Gallery, London.

116. RECLINING VENUS
1828 — Oil on canvas, 175 x 249 cm
Tate Gallery, London.

117. JESSICA
R.A. 1830 — Oil on canvas, 119.5 x 89 cm
Treasury and National Trust, Petworth House, Sussex

118. MUSIC PARTY, PETWORTH
c. 1835 — Oil on canvas, 21 x 90.5 cm
Tate Gallery, London.

119. YACHT APPROACHING THE COAST
c. 1835–40 — Oil on canvas, 102 x 142 cm
Tate Gallery, London.

120. THE 'SUN OF VENICE' GOING TO SEA
     R.A. 1843 — Oil on canvas, 61.5 x 92 cm
     Tate Gallery, London.

121. ST. BENEDETTO, LOOKING TOWARDS FUSINA
     R.A. 1843 — Oil on canvas, 61.5 x 92 cm
     Tate Gallery, London.

123. VENICE: SANTA MARIA DELLA SALUTE
R.A. 1844 — Oil on canvas, 61.5 x 92 cm
Tate Gallery, London.

124. PROCESSION OF BOATS WITH DISTANT SMOKE
c. 1845 — Oil on canvas, 90 x 120.5 cm

125. STORM AT VENICE
1840 — Watercolor, 21.8 x 31.8 cm
British Museum, London.

126. VENICE: THE GRAND CANAL, WITH ST. SIMEONE
PICCOLO: DUSK
1840 — Watercolor, 22.1 x 31.8 cm

127. STUDY OF SUNLIGHT
   1830 — Watercolor and gouache, 8.9 x 19 cm
   Victoria and Albert Museum, London.

128. VENICE: STORM AT SUNSET
   1840 — Watercolor and gouache, with scratching-out, 22.2 x 32 cm
   Fitzwilliam Museum, Cambridge.

129. SHORE SCENE: SUNSET
    c. 1830 — Watercolor and gouache, 9.7 x 18.9 cm
    Victoria and Albert Museum, London.

130. VENICE: CALM AT SUNRISE
    1840 — Watercolor, with some pen, 22.2 x 32.5 cm
    Fitzwilliam Museum, Cambridge.

131. ROOM IN VENICE
1839 — Watercolor, 24 x 30 cm
British Museum, London.

132. COLOR DIAGRAMS
British Museum, London.

133. LIGHT AND COLOUR (GOETHE'S THEORY) — THE MORNING
AFTER THE DELUGE — MOSES WRITING THE BOOK OF GENESIS
R.A. 1843 — Oil on canvas, 78.5 x 78.5 cm
Tate Gallery, London.

134. SHADE AND DARKNESS — THE EVENING OF THE DELUGE
R.A. 1843 — Oil on canvas, 78.5 x 78 cm
Tate Gallery, London.

135. UNDINE GIVING THE RING TO MASANIELLO, FISHERMAN OF NAPLES
R.A. 1846 — Oil on canvas, 79 x 79 cm
Tate Gallery, London.

136. THE ANGEL STANDING IN THE SUN
R.A. 1846 — Oil on canvas, 78.5 x 78.5 cm
Tate Gallery, London.

137. SKETCH OF A PHEASANT
c. 1815–20 — Watercolor over pencil, 22.3 x 34.5 cm
Ashmolean Museum, London.

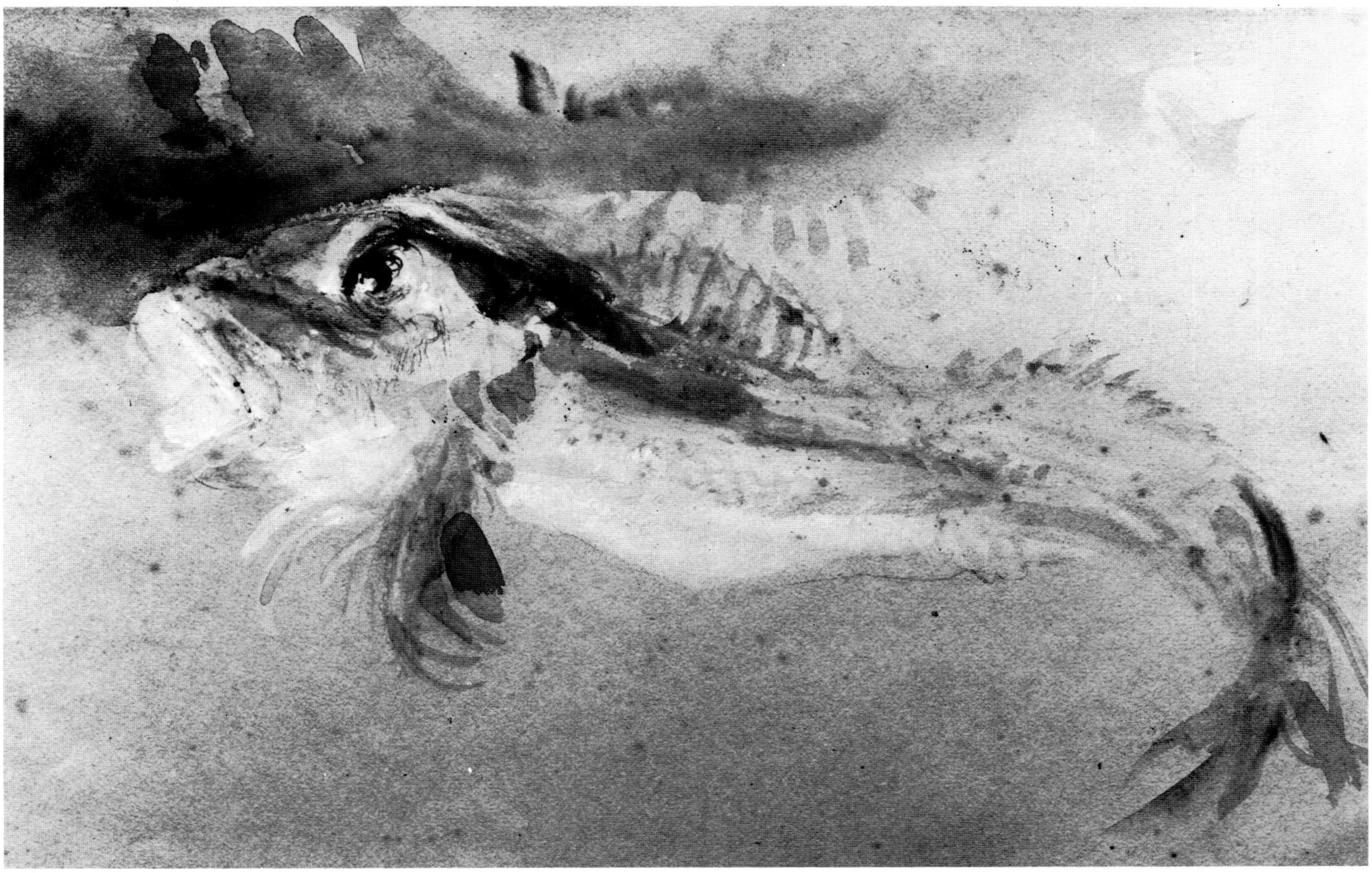

138. STUDY OF A GURNARD
c. 1840 — Watercolor and gouache, 19.3 x 27.6 cm
Vicoria and Albert Museum, London.

139. TOWN AT THE FOOT OF A HILL
1830–40 — Pencil, 14 x 19 cm
British Museum, London.

140. THE PALACE OF LA BELLE GABRIELLE
c. 1832–Pencil, pen and ink, and gouache, 13.6 x 19.2 cm
British Museum, London.

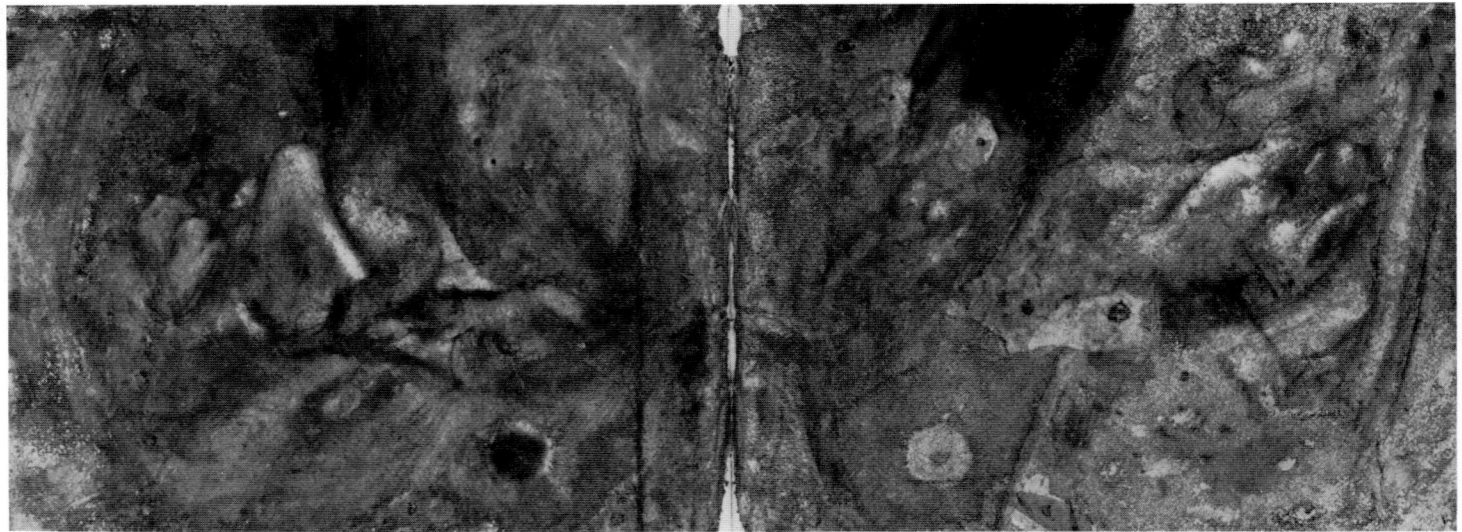

141. RECLINING COUPLE FROM SWISS SKETCH BOOK
c. 1802 — Pencil and gouache, 16 x 19 cm
British Museum, London.

142. EROTIC DRAWING
c. 1834 — pencil, 14 x 38 cm
British Museum, London.

VIII: ISOLATION (II): 1846–1851

I could not / Speak, and my eyes failed, I was neither / Living nor dead,
and I knew nothing / Looking into the heart of silence.

T.S. Eliot

The debate between the advocates of line and color has been a source of ferment throughout the history of Western painting, and rarely did it become more heated than during the Romantic era. Which was to be granted supreme power? There were a number of fundamental inferences to be drawn from this split. Was color to be confined and ''kept in line,'' so to speak, or could it assert its presence even as it helped to define forms? Was it supposed to consist of blended strokes that left a smooth, enamellike surface, or could the movement of brush against pigment leave tangible ''tracks'' in the paint and thereby register a painter's changing moods? Lastly, might color be given the freedom to do nothing but express? Beyond representation, beyond mere information, could color, like line, convey messages? All of these questions are as relevant today as they were then.

But a good deal more was involved than a difference in theory or technique. It was, and still is, a conflict between two sensibilities, indeed, two ways of understanding the world. According to one view, the senses came under the often tyrannical surveillance of thought; those in the other camp—including all self-respecting romantics—held that the scales tip in favor of sensation, that the senses tend to take over and carry one away. As Henry Fuseli put it in a lecture he delivered to the Royal Academy in 1802, ''When the object [of the arts] is to make sense the minister of the mind, ...*design*, in its most extensive...sense, is their basis; when they stoop to be the mere play-things, or debase themselves to be the debauchers of the senses, they make *colour* their insidious foundation.'' Even today, this assertion sums up an ideological viewpoint that usually lays great emphasis on order and hierarchy, as well as on moral values that have by no means fallen out of favor since Fuseli's era. (We might add that, in this particular case, it was put forward by a delightfully perverse painter who, in his own work, special-ized in horrifying, nightmarish visions.) Toward the end of the nineteenth century, this attitude was echoed in a naively Victorian statement by Charles Blanc, a member of the French Institute and an expert on the engravings of Rembrandt: ''Line is the male element in art, color, the female....Line must maintain its predominance over color, otherwise painting is on the road to ruin. It shall be painting's undoing as surely as Eve was mankind's'' (*Grammaire des Arts et du Dessin*). With statements of this sort in mind, even if purged of the Christian value system they implied, some ended up proclaiming a certain form of human expression ''degenerate art''.

When a painter's hand grows restless and anxious, lines automatically come apart at the seams, and well-defined, recognizable shapes give way to the hazy realm of fluidity and allusion.

A world bursting with unlimited potential—that is what romantic artists like Delacroix, Goya, and Turner were intent on exploring. Their efforts once again set in motion man's quest for the ephemeral. The forces of the Baroque emerged from oblivion to enjoy, if only for a brief period, a certain degree of currency. A few painters, working independently but sometimes utilizing similar techniques, set out to understand what they felt and turn it into something that could be both a medium and a message. However, this kind of communication involves a subjective process that brings the imagination into play. A pipedream, perhaps, but how irresistible a temptation nonetheless! Especially for Turner, a painter who was not as well suited as Goya or Delacroix to actually experi-ence it and, consequently, more inclined to imagine it. A painter who may have been hindered by an inability to feel it within himself, thus more consumed with a desire to re-create it elsewhere.

In Turner's paintings, this transmutation was brought about through light—no other artist had ever raised light to such a pitch of violence—and unrestrained use of color. At times he kept his palette within the bounds of representation deemed proper by a certain society at a certain point in history, but he could just as easily flout convention if it brought him closer to achieving his goals. Now circumspect, now exuberant, depending on his mood or outlook, Turner's brushwork has a vigor that never seems contrived or strained. Sensation is by nature effusive, especially for a Romantic intent on excess. Everything in painting is a matter of infinitesimal doses, of imperceptible nuances. To paraphrase Charles Baudelaire, a great painting that is commensurate with and true to the sensation that inspired it ''must be brought forth like a world.''

A person's tastes are invariably rooted in predispositions, in an indwelling attraction of one kind or another. Was Turner's unflagging interest in topographical art dictated by nothing more than professional circumstances or financial need, or was he responding to an irresistible urge from deep within his unconscious? Newport, Caernarvon, Richmond, Rosehill, Fonthill, Chillon, Pembroke, Petworth, Norham—the castles, fortresses, and estates Turner always came back to, especially in his watercolors, are legion. His lifelong delight was to draw their towers, facades, and porticos in meticulous, but expressive detail, to capture them in different seasons and at different times of day, from dawn to dusk.

Though probably not the most prominent of these subjects, Norham Castle was the one that sustained the painter's interest over the longest period of time. A first, sharply defined rendering of the castle appeared in 1797, then in a painstaking watercolor that was exhibited at the Royal Academy the following year. In 1801, Turner stopped on his way to Scotland to make a series of pencil and watercolor studies—some tranquil, others dramatic—that place the light source behind the castle. He returned to the subject in 1815 in an engraving for the *Liber Studiorum* and again in a particularly bold watercolor in which he juxtaposed red, blue, and yellow with unprecedented freedom and fluidity. Norham reappeared in 1831, with the sun breaking through the clouds and the iridescent orange and mauve mist, while reflections skim the surface of the river. Turner sang Norham's praises (ill.151) for one last time between 1835 and 1840 in a dazzling oil: some lustrous, shimmering yellow, some translucent blue, a few strokes of red for some stray cattle. This wonderful castle seems to embody everything the painter longed for; it was his oasis of tranquility, his haven of security, and his New Jerusalem rolled into one.

Rocky Bay (1828-1830), a blend of evasive forms and unresolved light, offers another view of this mythic embodiment of serenity where all of Turner's more baneful longings faded into muffled, peaceful silence. The scenes (ill.119,150) depicted in *Rocky Bay, Yacht Approaching the Coast,* and *Stormy Sea with Dolphins* tell of a world before Genesis, a world in which water, air, and light have not yet been separated from one another. Ships, dolphins, and sea monsters seem to spring from the paint itself, as though messengers of foreboding from some distant land.

In his book on landscape drawing, Alexander Cozens suggested that, just as Leonardo da Vinci had noted that an artist should try and pick out recognizable shapes in the stains of mildewed walls, a painter should compose a landscape as spontaneously as possible, picking out and elaborating on elements as his brush moves across the canvas or sheet of paper. No doubt Turner was familiar with Cozens's theory; he, too, was intent on tapping the potential of his medium to the fullest. Although chance events in the paint could stimulate his imagination in the way Cozens described, they always brought him back to that ''golden Orient'' he perpetually longed for. It is said that he suffered from an eye disorder, but he saw well enough to make out slashes, knots, and fissures in the wet pigment and develop them into identifiable forms. Turner was so intrigued by the purely physical aspect of his art, so painstaking a craftsman, that he seemed to abhor a smooth, lustrous surface, now laying on a thick impasto, now digging into the paint with the tip of his brush. He was partial to palette knives, which allowed him to scrape his oils and create a dynamic play of peaks and valleys. But relief for Turner was more than just a way of catching light. His handling of this techinque was so delicate and felicitous that it took on the quality of an unexpected, but indispensible ''happening.'' It registered, not just the movement of his hand, but his restiveness, his ''slips,'' whether intentional or not. It was his way of reaching another dimension where meaning is conveyed through a transcendent form of communication. Sensation is a private, ineffable phenomenon. Any attempt to break through that barrier of solitude means having to cast an infinitely complex, at times hermetic net of metaphor and association that might capture the imagination of viewers yet unborn.

Rocky Bay (1828-1830)

Although completed at different dates over a nine-year period, three of Turner's paintings may be considered a group in that they are all uncommonly ambitious, even for Turner: *Fire at Sea; Snow Storm: Steam-boat off a Harbour's Mouth Making Signals in Shallow Water, and Going By the Lead. The Author was in This Storm on the Night the Ariel Left Harwich;* and *Rain, Steam, and Speed—The Great Western Railway.*

The product of a vexed and haunted imagination, *Fire at Sea* develops a structure with which Turner had already experimented: four triangles, their tips joined more or less at the center of the canvas. Sharp outlines have been eaten away by jagged, windswept clouds and smoke. But there is a tragic side to the horrible scene, for the storm-tossed raft is locked in a hopeless struggle with the unbridled forces of nature. Another triangle is formed by a writhing cluster of panic-stricken women who are clinging to the smallest bit of rough surface and using their last ounce of strength to save their children from the raging swells. Fire is indistinguishable from water; the conflagration has set the sea ablaze and caused it to change color. A dense shower of flaming sparks is raining down from the sky like the fringe and tassels of a theater curtain. A few bewildered men, flung back to the edge of the planks, are making absurd signals while propped up against their last refuge, a useless mast without a sail. This is not the *Raft of the Medusa* (1819), in which Géricault tried to raise a public furor over the incompetence of the French maritime administration. In Turner's painting, man has been found guilty and placed at the mercy of elements that have run amok. Yet, he rebels against destiny, he protests against the unjust punishment that has been meted out to him. Bristling with derision and pessimism. a theatrical counterpart of his equally theatrical *Fallacies of Hope, Fire at Sea* has—to its credit or detriment, depending on one's point of view—a universal quality worthy of Victor Hugo.

Here we catch a glimpse of the heroic rebel that lay within this uncouth little man whom critics dismissed as capricious. True, his overriding concern was to meet the challenges of his craft, but deep down he also longed to respect tradition. There are many aritsts whose work reflects yearnings, innate inadequacies, or setbacks met along life's path. Turner's oeuvre speaks of the ruthless struggle between man and a hostile nature that threatens to overhwelm him. Like the dog Goya painted on the walls of the Quinta del Sordo, Turner took a lone stand against death in true Romantic fashion. What can life mean when its only certainty is death? That is a question people have always asked, and for which they have never had anything but vague and hesitant answers.

As we contemplate these figments of Turner's imagination, what other meaning can we give to the little boat in *Snow Storm* (1842), adrift in a pyramid of light, crushed by triangles that whirl about like the sails of a Portugese (ill.143) windmill in a prophetic wind? What other meaning could the nightmarish *Rain, Steam, and Speed* have, with its (ill.146) frenzied locomotive hurtling toward us at full speed amid an atmosphere laden with doom? Especially when, in a moment of mockery, humor, or metaphor, the painter made a point of adding an absurd hare, which is madly dashing to scamper away in time from the path of the oncoming engine.

"In the course of these descriptions," writes Jean–Jacques Mayoux, "I have had occasion to speak of *Einfühlung*, or 'empathy,' that kind of sinewy imagination which is part and parcel of the dynamics of creation. To discover mighty dramas such as these within one's sinews, they have to have been put there first. Turner paid dearly for his." When critics discuss paintings like *Rain, Steam, and Speed*, they recall how he took whatever measures were necessary to experience things firsthand, whether it meant spending hours observing storms at sea while lashed to a ship's mast, or leaning out of a train window, the better to feel gusts of wind slapping against his face.

His predilection for railroads attracted him to the birdge at Maidenhead that Isambard Kingdom Brunel, one of (ill.146) the great architects of the day, built for the Great Western Railway. Some believe that the painting commemorated the opening of the Bristol–Exeter extension, which, it so happens, took place in 1844. It has also been suggested that the hare running in front of the train is simply Turner's way of comparing the speeds of animal and machine. But there must be more to the puffs of steam driven by the rainstorm and to the "Firefly Class" locomotive (the most advanced type of its day) than a glorification of modern day machinery. The painting itself says more than that. One need only note the impression of receding space created by the elongated bridge to sense that this slowing mass is the train of death bearing down on whoever sees it approaching.

Even if realism was conceivably one of Turner's aims, this does not mean that his paintings dealt with "reality" as we know it. He painted that snowstorm and rainstorm in a way no one had ever seen them before. To the extent they were conjured up through the artifices of art, they had never even existed. Turner had finally succeeded in conveying sensation through paint, and with what violence! Imagination had triumphed over the code of representation, with uncanny, "terrible" results, to quote Disraeli. A new horizon had once again opened up to art in the nineteenth century, one from which people had been cut off since the age of the Baroque. It was an approach that painters were to probe and exploit for may decades to come. Paul Klee later wrote in *Theory of Modern Art*, "Art does not reproduce the visible world; it makes it visible…" As he painted his *Improvisations*, Kandinsky did not have to rely on nature as a point of reference in order to convey the organic vitality of the earth, its whirlwinds, its frenzied outbursts, its effusivenees.

Death had deprived him of his closest friends and old age was creeping up on him, but there may have been other reasons for Turner's increasing dejection and aloofness at this time. Once again he sought refuge in "covering up." He maintained his official household and gallery, but they were closely guarded secrets. In 1846, he rented a house in Chelsea and placed it in the name of Sophia Caroline Booth. His anguish was so profound that he felt compelled to change his identity. Is there symbolic meaning here, or was this simply a wish to drop out of sight? By taking Mrs. Booth's name while living in her house, did he want others to regard him as a kind of parent, or was it his old, unconscious yearning to play the part of a son? A concern for keeping up appearances cannot fully account for this bizarre comedy of confused images and identities. Mrs. Booth may not have been a model of refinement, but at least she was an attentive, motherly companion (and, to Turner's immense satisfaction, a frugal housekeeper). Hannah Danby, Sarah's niece, occupied the house on Queen Anne Street most of the time, and the charming, sensitive Elizabeth Rigby (later Lady Eastlake), one of the artist's admirers, left us a heartrending account of her visit to Turner's London residence on May 20, 1846.

Painting was Turner's sole reason for living. His canvases mattered more to him than anything else, and money was his most prized possession. His works were by now, as the ex–Mrs. Ruskin put it, "desolate in the extreme," a condition that no doubt reflected the delapidated state into which Turner himself had fallen. He had become a disillusioned, melancholy man who made frequent changes in his will. His teeth troubled him, and toward the end of his life he could take nothing but milk and rum. Alcohol did its insidious work. On December 19, 1851, seeing some light breaking through the overcast skies, he managed to struggle out of bed and stumbled into a ray of sunshine. (The last detail has prompted symbolic interpretations from every quarter.) Turner's body was taken to the house on Queen Anne Street and lay in state in his gallery. The funeral took place on December 30, 1851, in St. Paul's Cathedral, and his remains were buried in the crypt, along with those of Sir Joshua Reynolds and Sir Thomas Lawrence. Upon his return from Sir Thomas's funeral, Turner wrote to George Jones about his fellow Academician, ''However, it is something to feel that gifted talent can be acknowledged by the many who yesterday waded up to their knees in snow and muck to see the funeral pomp swelled up by the carriages of the great...'' At last Turner achieved in death what he had longed for his entire life: recognition. Not entirely, however, for Queen Victoria had not knighted or decorated him, while others considerably less gifted than he were so honored.

''Art's a rum business,'' Turner often remarked, and nothing could provide more convincing and depressing proof than the intrigue occasioned by his bequest. The stakes were high indeed. Not counting real estate, the artist's fortune was valued at 140,000 pounds and, according to the catalogue of 1856, included more than 19,000 paintings, watercolors, and drawings.

On three essential points Turner never wavered:

1. That *Dido Building Carthage* and *Sun Rising through Vapour* should be exhibited between Claude Lorrain's *Seaport: The Embarkation of the Queen of Sheba* and *The Mill*. His executors duly delivered the paintings to the National Gallery within one year after Turner's death, as stipulated in the will, and there held in escrow until the will was settled. The two paintings hang today in the National Gallery precisely as the artist wished.

2. That all finished pictures should be bequeathed to the nation, provided that they be put on permanent display in a museum to be built and maintained at state expense. The museum was to be completed within ten years of the artist's demise; until then, they were to be kept at his gallery on Queen Anne Street. Upkeep and custodial services were to be paid out from the estate. If these provisions could not be carried out and the finished pictures could not be exhibited as prescribed on Queen Anne Street, everything, including real estate and personal property, was to be sold.

3. That the money from the above sale, should it take place, be added to the fortune he left to a ''Charitable Institution'' for ''the Maintenance and support of Poor and Decayed Male Artists being born in England and of English parents only and lawful issue.''

Turner's will was immediately contested. The artist was not in his right mind toward the end of his life, claimed his distant (and slighted) relatives. His executors, however, declared the will valid and made preparations for a major exhibition of his work in the Queen Anne Street gallery. Turner's ably advised next of kin sought refuge in the jungle of legal proceedings and played the executors' lack of tenacity to advantage. Years later, the parties involved worked out an agreement in which not one of Turner's wishes was respected.

''First,'' writes John Walker, ''the executors gave up all the cash in the estate. The Royal Academy, to which Turner had conditionally left 1000 pounds, ended up with 20,000, and, except for a few individual bequests which were honored, the relatives took the rest. The charitable institution, Turner's lifelong dream, for which he had toiled and saved, was never realized. The executors also gave the relatives the house on Queen Anne Street, frustrating Turner's wish to keep all his pictures in one place until the terms of his bequest were fulfilled. 'What is the use of them but together?' he had asked repeatedly. Only if they were kept in a series, he felt, would the key to their meaning be discernible. This was his prinicpal aspiration. It is still unfulfilled...''

''There was to be a further infraction of his will. In bequeathing his paintings to the nation, Turner had made a significant division between 'finished' and 'unfinished' pictures, a distinction which must have seemed important to him...Vice–Chancellor Kindersley in the Court of Chancery, however, decreed that 'all the pictures, Drawings and Sketches by the Testator's hand—without any distinction of finished and unfinished—are to be deemed as well given for the benefit of the public.'''

A violation of Turner's rights, to be sure, but one that preserved the aesthetic unity of his work.

143. SNOW STORM — STEAM-BOAT OFF A HARBOUR'S MOUTH MAKING SIGNALS IN SHALLOW WATER, AND GOING BY THE LEAD. THE AUTHOR WAS IN THIS STORM ON THE NIGHT THE ARIEL LEFT HARWICH
R.A. 1842 — Oil on canvas, 91.5 x 122 cm
Tate Gallery, London.

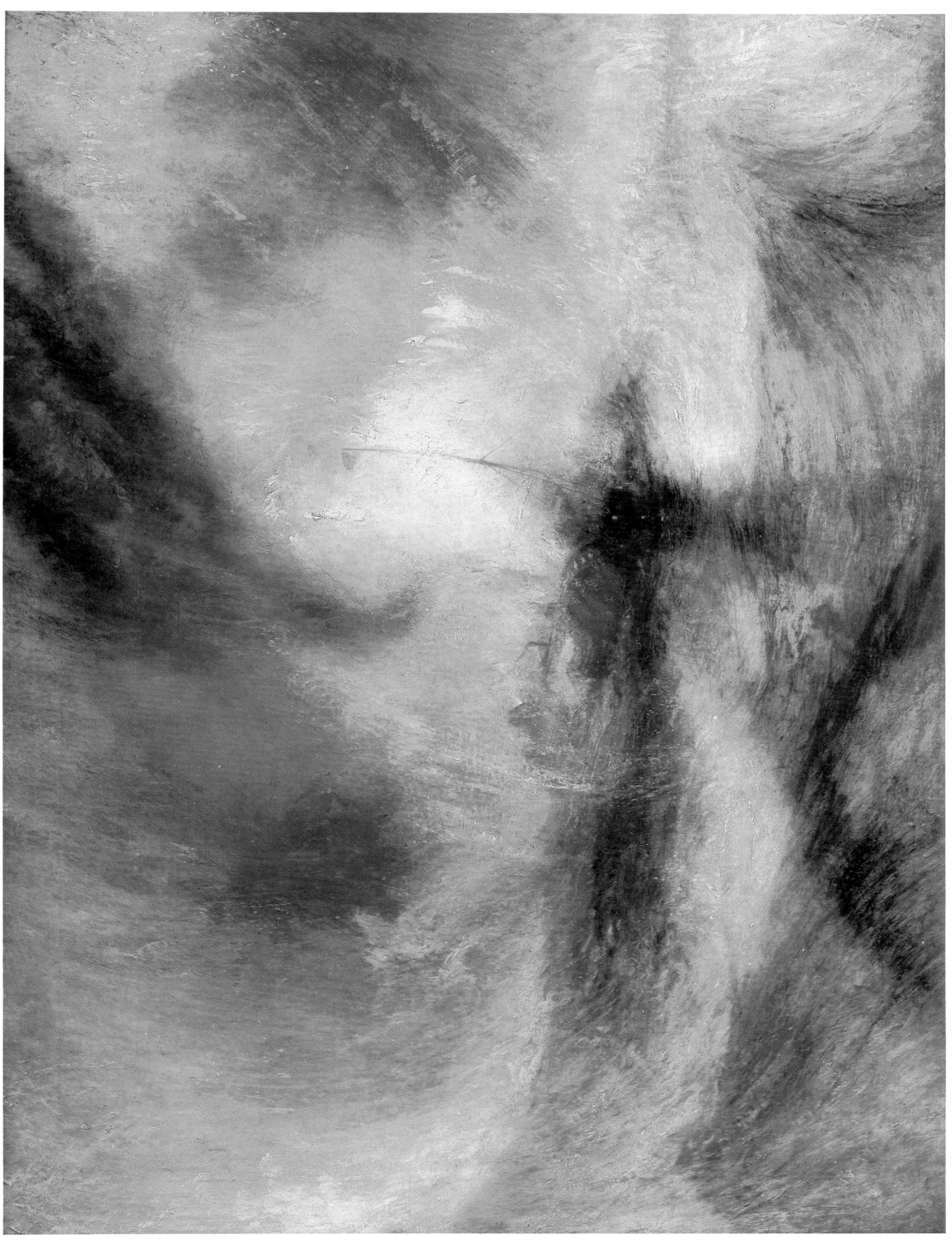

144. PHRYNE GOING TO THE PUBLIC BATH AS VENUS —
DEMOSTHENES TAUNTED BY AESCHINES
R.A. 1838 — Oil on canvas, 180.5 x 165 cm
Tate Gallery, London.

145. BACCHUS AND ARIADNE
R.A. 1840 — Oil on canvas, 79 x 79 cm
Tate Gallery, London.

147

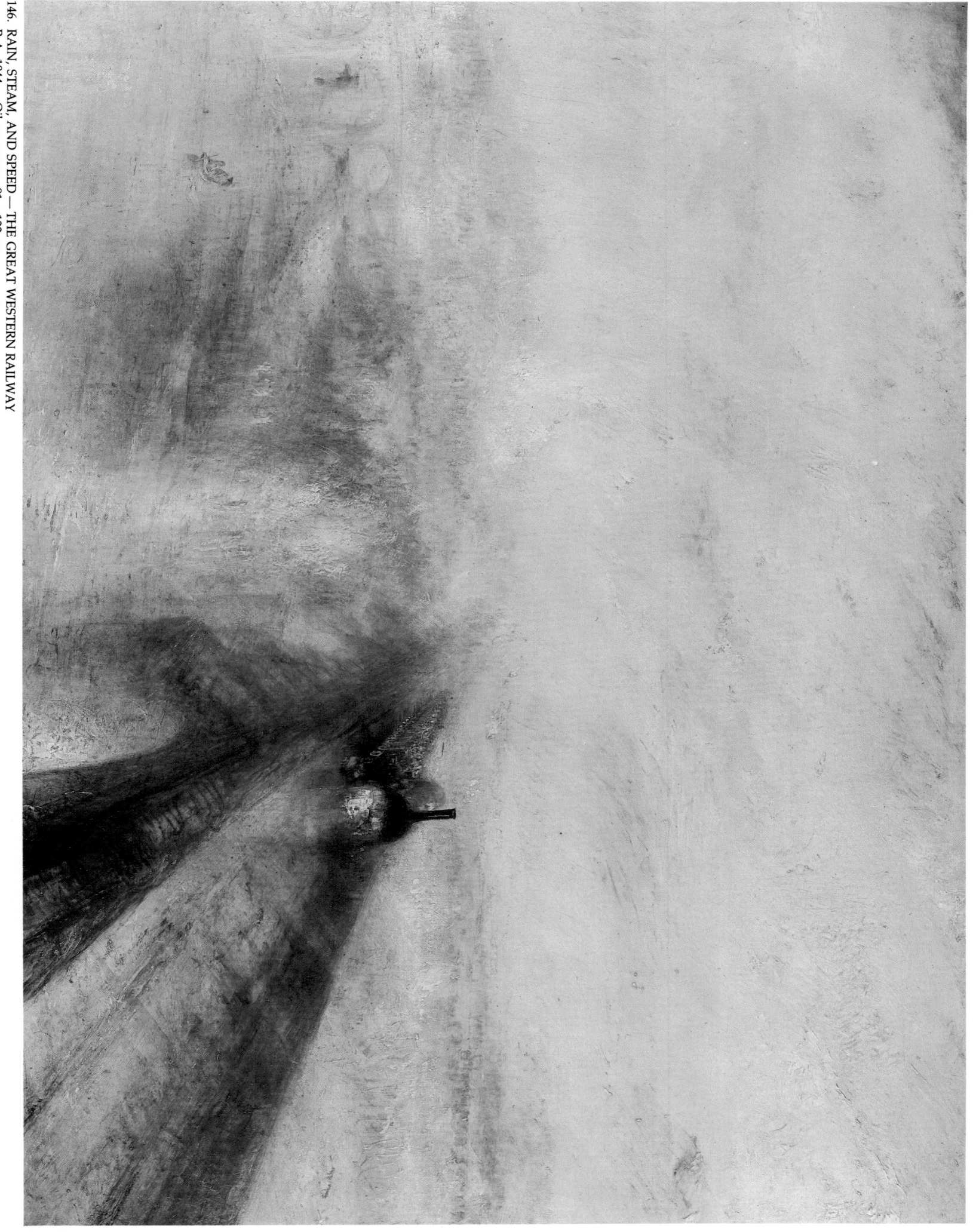

146. RAIN, STEAM, AND SPEED — THE GREAT WESTERN RAILWAY
R.A. 1844 — Oil on canvas, 91 x 122 cm
National Gallery, London

147. A WRECK, WITH FISHING BOATS
c. 1840–45 — Oil on canvas, 91.5 x 122 cm
Tate Gallery, London.

148. ANCIENT ROME: AGRIPPINA LANDING WITH THE ASHES OF GERMANICUS. THE TRIUMPHAL BRIDGE AND PALACE OF THE CAESARS RESTORED
R.A. 1839 — Oil on canvas, 91.5 x 122 cm
Tate Gallery, London.

149. WHALERS (BOILING BLUBBER) ENTANGLED IN THE FLAW ICE,
ENDEAVORING TO EXTRICATE THEMSELVES
R.A. 1846 — Oil on canvas, 90 x 120 cm
Tate Gallery, London.

150. STORMY SEA WITH DOLPHINS
c. 1835–40 — Oil on canvas, 91 x 102 cm
Tate Gallery, London

151. NORHAM CASTLE, SUNRISE
c. 1835–40 — Oil on canvas, 91 x 122 cm
Tate Gallery, London.

152. VISIT TO THE TOMB
     R.A. 1850 — Oil on canvas, 91.5 x 122 cm
     Tate Gallery, London.

153. SUNRISE, WITH A BOAT BETWEEN HEADLANDS
c. 1835–40 — Oil on canvas, 91.5 x 122 cm
Tate Gallery, London.

154. A LANDSCAPE WITH A RIVER AND A BAY IN THE DISTANCE
Between 1835 and 1840 — Oil on canvas, 94 x 123 cm
Musée du Louvre, Paris.

155. TANCARVILLE, WITH THE TOWN OF QUILLEBOEUF
c. 1832 — Gouache on blue paper, 14 x 19.1 cm
British Museum, London.

156. SHOAL, ON THE SEINE
c. 1832 — Gouache, with some pen, 13.9 x 19.1 cm
British Museum, London.

157. ORLÉANS
c. 1826–1830 — Watercolor and gouache, with pen, on blue paper,
13.6 x 18.9 cm
Ashmolean Museum, Oxford.

158. CHÂTEAU OF AMBOISE
c. 1826–1830 — Watercolor and gouache, with pen, on blue paper,
13.6 x 18.8 cm
Ashmolean Museum, Oxford.

159. BLOIS
c. 1826–1830 — Watercolor and gouache, with pen, on blue paper, 13.5 x 18.3 cm
Ashmolean Museum, Oxford.

160. ST. JULIAN'S, TOURS
c. 1826–1830 — Pencil, watercolor and gouache, on blue paper, 12 x 18.4 cm
Ashmolean Museum, Oxford.

161. HAVRE, TOWER OF FRANCIS I: TWILIGHT OUTSIDE THE PORT
c. 1832 — gouache on blue paper, 14 x 19.2 cm
British Museum, London.

162. PARIS: MARCHÉ AUX FLEURS AND PONT-AU-CHANGE
c. 1832 — Watercolor and gouache on blue paper, 13.9 x 19 cm
British Museum, London.

163. HONFLEUR
c. 1832 — Watercolor and gouache, with some pen and brown color
on blue paper, 14 x 19.1 cm
British Museum, London.

164. ROUEN: THE WEST FRONT OF THE CATHEDRAL
c. 1832 — Watercolor and gouache, with some pen, on blue paper,
14 x 19.4 cm
British Museum, London.

165. LYONS
   c. 1846 — Watercolor with some gouache, 24.1 x 30.5 cm
   Victoria and Albert Museum, London.

166. LAKE OF ZUG: EARLY MORNING
   1843 — Watercolor, 29.8 x 46.6 cm
   Metropolitan Museum, New York.

167. BACHARACH
c. 1840 — Watercolor and gouache over pencil, on white paper,
18.4 x 24.1 cm
Fitzwilliam Museum, Cambridge.

168. STORM IN A SWISS PASS ('FIRST BRIDGE ABOVE ALTDORF')
1845 — Watercolor and surface scratching, 29 x 47 cm
Whitworth Art Gallery, University of Manchester

169. PARIS: HÔTEL DE VILLE AND PONT D'ARCOLE
c. 1832 — Watercolor and gouache on blue paper, 13.9 x 19 cm
British Museum, London.

170. LUCERNE: MOONLIGHT
1843 — Watercolor, 29 x 47.6 cm
British Museum, London.

171. THE EVENING STAR
c. 1830 — Oil on canvas, 92.5 x 123 cm
National Gallery, London.

173. SAILING SHIP IN A STORM
After 1830 — Gouache, 16 x 19 cm
British Museum, London.

CCCLXIV 394

172. STUDY OF A FIRE
Watercolor, 23 x 32 cm
British Museum, London.

174. MAUVE SEA
Watercolor, 16 x 22 cm
British Museum, London.

177. SKY AND SEA
c. 1835 — Watercolor, 48.7 x 65.5 cm
British Museum, London.

175. GREY SEA
Watercolor
British Museum, London.

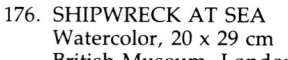

178. FIGURES IN A PINK ATMOSPHERE
Watercolor, 19 x 25 cm
British Museum, London.

176. SHIPWRECK AT SEA
Watercolor, 20 x 29 cm
British Museum, London.

BIOGRAPHY

1775 April 23: Joseph Mallord William Turner born to William Turner and his wife, Mary Marshall. A barber and wigmaker by profession, Turner runs a shop in London's Covent Garden district.

1778 Birth of a daughter, Mary Ann, who dies in 1786 after a serious illness.

1785-1786 Young Turner spends a year at his uncle's home in Brentford, Middlesex. First sketches.

1789 "Oxford" sketchbook. Admitted to the Royal Academy Schools in December. Studies with the painter Thomas Malton, who specializes in architectural subjects. Believed to have studied drawing in the studio of the architect Hardwick.

1790 Exhibits first watercolor, The Archbishop's Palace, Lambeth, at the Royal Academy.

1791-1792 Sketches and drawings at Bath, Bristol, Malmesbury, and gorges along the Avon. First excursion into Wales, the Wye Valley, and central and southern England.

1793-1794 The Society of Arts awards Turner the "Greater Silver Pallet." Meets Dr. Thomas Monro, for whom he and Thomas Girtin copy and color drawings by J. R. Cozens and other artists. Continues this work for three years. Works in the Midlands and contemplates the possibility of engravings based on his drawings. Drawings commissioned by Viscount Malden.

1795 Meets Richard Colt Hoare de Stouzhead in Wiltshire. Travels to Wales and the Isle of Wight in June and July.

1796 Exhibits ten watercolors and his first oil painting at the Royal Academy. Drawings commissioned by Sir Richard Colt Hoare.

1797 Excursion into Yorkshire, Northumberland, and the Lake District. Drawings commissioned by the Lascelles family.

1798 Travels to Wales.

1799 Elected an Associate Member of the Royal Academy. Moves into a house at 64 Harley Street. Liaison with Sarah Danby begins. Another trip to Wales, then proceeds to Lancashire. Watercolors of Fonthill (1800) commissioned by William Beckford.

1800 Turner's mother admitted to Bethlem Hospital, London's insane asylum. Begins to publish poetry intended to accompany paintings exhibited at the Royal Academy.

1801 First trip to Scotland.

1802 February 12: Elected a full member of the Royal Academy at age twenty-seven. With the signing of the Peace of Amiens, Turner travels to Switzerland and France. Sketches at the Louvre.

1803 Walter Fawkes, who befriends the artist and later commissions a number of watercolors, buys his first Turner.

1804 Sets up a private gallery at 64 Harley Street.

1806 His friend W. F. Wells persuades him to begin Liber Studiorum. Both consider it an excellent way of getting Turner's work into the public eye. Sends two paintings to the first exhibition of the Royal Academy.

1807 June: First installment of Liber Studiorum published, but work is not completed until 1819. Appointed professor of perspective at the Royal Academy.

1808 Spends some time at Tabley Hall, the Cheshire estate of Sir John Leicester, a prominent collector of paintings.

1809 Meets Lord Egremont for the first time and spends some time at Petworth.

1810 Visits Farnley Hall, Walter Fawkes's Yorkshire estate. Moves to 47 Queen Anne Street West.

1811 Finally teaches his first classes in perspective at the Royal Academy. Travels through Dorset, Devon, Cornwall, and Somerset, sketching for his planned series of engravings, Picturesque Views of the Southern Coast of England (1824). Sells the house he had bought in Hammersmith and draws up plans for Sandycombe Lodge in Twickenham, which is completed in 1813.

1815 Peace with France, making travel in Europe possible once again. Drawings commissioned by John Fuller (1820).

1817 First trip to Belgium, the Rhineland, Holland. On his return, completes fifty-one watercolors of views along the Rhine. The entire series is purchased by Sir Walter Fawkes. Illustrates Surtees's History of Durham.

1818 Begins a series of watercolors for his Picturesque Tour in Italy, based on drawings by James Hakewill.

1819 First trip to Italy. Turner's discovery of light here is to have a far-reaching effect on his work. Sir John Leicester exhibits eight of Turner's paintings in London. In 1819

and 1820, Walter Fawkes exhibits in his home a large group of watercolors, including those of Farnley Hall which Turner had begin in 1815.

1820 Sets up a more spacious gallery in his Queen Anne Street house.

1821 Trip to France, with stops at Paris, Dieppe, Le Havre and Rouen.

1822 Takes part in the "Splendid Drawings" show arranged by the publisher W. B. Cooke. Intrudes on the celebrations held in honor of George IV's official visit to Edinburgh. Illustrates works by Scott, Byron, and Moore for Walter Fawkes (1840).

1823 Commissioned to paint The Battle of Trafalgar for St. James's Palace; completed in May, 1824. Begins work on Rivers of England (1827).

1824 Travels through northern, northeastern and southern England.

1825 October 25: Death of Walter Fawkes. Begins various studies for the Little Liber (1830) and Rivers of Europe (1834).

1826 Trip to France: the Meuse, the Moselle, Brittany, and the Loire. Begins illustrations for Samuel Rogers's poem Italy (1828), which is published in 1830. A series of engravings, Picturesque Views in England and Wales, commissioned by Charles Heath; its ninety-six plates are published between 1827 and 1838. Thomas Lupton's engravings of The Ports of England (1828), based on Turner's drawings. Turner sells Sandycombe Lodge.

1827 Spends time with John Nash on the Isle of Wight. Visits Lord Egremont at Petworth; Turner a frequent guest there until Lord Egremont's death in 1837. Walter Fawkes's collection scattered.

1828 Teaches his last class at the Royal Academy. Second trip to Italy.

1829 September 21: Death of Turner's father.

1830 Spends time in the Midlands. Sketches for Picturesque Views of the East Coast of England.

1831 Travels across Scotland. Meets Walter Scott, whose poems the artist is about to illustrate.

1832 Completes twenty-four drawings for Finden's Landscape Illustrations of the Bible (1835) and seventeen ornamental pieces for the Murray edition of Byron's collected works. He had already done seven full-page illustrations for the same author and publisher around 1823-1824.

1833 Spends time in Paris. Extensive travels to the Baltic, Berlin, Prague and probably Venice.

1834 Travels along the Meuse, the Moselle and the Rhine. Goes frequently to Margate to visit Sophia Carolyn Booth. Illustrations for Milton's Poetical Works.

1835 Drawings for poems by Thomas Campbell and White's View in India.

1836 Travels to France, Switzerland, and the Val d'Aoste with H. A. J. Munro of Novar. Ruskin's first letter to Turner, containing his unpublished reply to Rev. Eagles's attacks in Blackwood's Magazine.

1837 November 11: Death of Lord Egremont. Resigns as professor of perspective at the Royal Academy. Death of the architect Sir John Soane.

1840 Meets Ruskin for the first time. Trip to Holland and Germany; spends time in Venice, returns by way of Austria and Germany, where he sketches Walhalla.

1841-1842 Trips to Switzerland.

1843 First volume of Ruskin's Modern Painters published.

1844 Travels to Switzerland, along the Rhine; visits Heidelberg. Meets Charles Dickens.

1845 The president of the Royal Academy is taken ill, and Turner takes over his duties temporarily. Brief stay at Boulogne-sur-Mer, proceeds to Dieppe and the coast of Picardy in autumn.

1846 Rents lodgings in Mrs. Booth's name at 119 Cheyne Walk, Chelsea, where he lives the life of a recluse. Known to neighborhood residents as "Admiral Booth" or "Captain Booth."

1851 December 19: Turner dies in Chelsea. Buried in St. Paul's Cathedral on December 30. Turner bequeaths his collection, property, and fortune to the nation, provided that a museum be built and all of his works exhibited in one place. This wish was not carried out.

The dates of Turner's illustrations are taken from Andrew Wilton's invaluable catalogue of the artist's work. The date in parentheses indicates the year in which the final version of a planned or ongoing work was published. This, I believe, will help give the reader an idea of the intensity with which Turner worked.

Concise Bibliography

Monographs and Other Works

THORNBURY, Walter *The Life of J. M. W. Turner, R. A.* 2 vol. London, 1862.

RUSKIN, John. *The Modern Painters.* 6 vol. London, 1888.

RUSKIN, John. *Works.* Edited by E. T. Cook and Alexander Wedderburn. London: George Allen, 1903–1912.

FARINGTON, Joseph. *The Farrington Diary.* Edited by James Greig. 8 vol. London: Hutchinson and Company, 1922-1928.

BRION, Marcel. *Turner.* Rieder, 1929.

QUENNEL, Peter. *John Ruskin. The Portrait of a Prophet.* New York: Viking Press, 1949.

FINBERG, A. J. *The life of J. M. W. Turner R. A.* Second edition revised with supplement by Helda F. Finberg. The Clarendon Press: Oxford, 1961.

ROTHENSTEIN, John and BUTLIN, Martin. *Turner.* New York and London: George Braziller, 1964.

ROTHENSTEIN, John. *Turner.* Le Musée Personnel: Paris, 1965.

LINDSAY, Jack. *Turner. His Life and Work.* Harper and Row: New York, 1966.

GAGE, John. *Colour in Turner: Poetry and Truth.* Studio Vista, 1969.

MAYOUX, Jean-Jacques. *La peinture anglaise. De Hogarth aux Préraphaélites.* Skira: Geneva, 1972.

GAUNT, William. *L'univers de Turner. Les carnets de dessins.* Henri Screpel: Paris, 1974.

SELZ, Jean. *Turner.* Flammarion: Paris, 1975.

WILKINSON, Gerald. *Turner Sketches, 1789-1820.* Barrie and Jenkins, Ltd.: London, 1977.

BUTLIN, Andrew. *J. M. W. Turner, Vie et oeuvre. Catalogues des peintures et aquarelles.* Office du Livre, Fribourg. Ed. Vilo: Paris, 1979.

CLAY, Jean. *Le Romantisme.* Hachette Réalités: Paris, 1980.

GAGE, John. *Collected Correspondance of J. M. W. Turner.* Clarendon Press: Oxford, 1980.

GOETHE, J. W. *Traité des couleurs.* Triades: Paris, 1980.

MARTINET, Marie-Madeleine. *Art et nature en Grande-Bretagne au XVIIIe siècle. De l'harmonie classique du premier romantisme.* Aubier, Montaigne Ed.: Paris, 1980.

ROUVE, Pierre. *Turner.* Siloé Ed.: Paris 1980.

WALKER, John. *Turner.* Editions Cercle d'Art, Paris and Harry N. Abrams, New York, 1980.

PROVENANCE OF PHOTOGRAPHS

WALTER ART GALLERY, BALTIMORE
black and white: 56.

MUSEUM OF FINE ARTS, BOSTON
black and white: 108.

FITZWILLIAM MUSEUM, CAMBRIDGE
black and white photographs: 14, 128, 130, 176 and page 8.

NATIONAL MARITIME MUSEUM, GREENWICH
color photograph: 69.

INDIANAPOLIS MUSEUM OF ART
black and white photographs: 4, 20 and page 80.

UNIVERSITY OF LIVERPOOL
color photograph: 35.

BRITISH MUSEUM, LONDON
color photographs: 1, 6, 63, 82-89, 125, 126, 131, 132, 155, 156, 169, 170, 172-178.
black and white photogaphs: 2, 3, 5, 7, 8, 9, 10, 11, 12, 13, 15, 16, 23, 24, 25, 27, 28, 39, 40, 43, 44, 59, 60, 61, 62, 67, 100, 101, 102, 104, 105, 139, 140, 141, 142, 161, 162, 163, 164 and pages 11, 19, 93, 94.

COURTAULD INSTITUTE, LONDON
black and white photograph: 41.

NATIONAL GALLERY, LONDON
color photographs: 32, 96, 99, 110, 171.
black and white photographs: 31, 53, 55.

NATIONAL PORTRAIT GALLERY, LONDON
black and white photograph: page 17.

TATE GALLERY, LONDON
color photographs: 18, 21, 29, 47, 51, 52, 57, 58, 64, 70, 78, 81, 90, 95, 113, 114, 118, 119, 124, 133, 136, 143, 147, 150, 151.
black and white photographs: 19, 33, 37, 38, 48, 49, 50, 54, 65, 66, 68, 71, 73, 74, 76, 79, 80, 91, 92, 93, 94, 97, 98, 111, 112, 115, 116, 120, 121, 122, 123, 134, 135, 144, 145, 148, 149, 152, 153 and pages 2, 33, 48, 114, 142.

VICTORIA AND ALBERT MUSEUM, LONDON
black and white photographs: 17, 22, 26, 103, 127, 129, 138, 165 and pages 9, 34.

WHITWORTH ART GALLERY, MANCHESTER
black and white photograph: 168.

METROPOLITAN MUSEUM OF ART, NEW YORK
black and white photograph: 166.

ASHMOLEAN MUSEUM, OXFORD
black and white photographs: 45, 137, 157, 158, 159, 160 and page 95.

MUSÉES NATIONAUX, PARIS
color photograph: 154.

RAPHO, PARIS
color photograph: 146.

NATIONAL TRUST, PETWORTH HOUSE
black and white photographs: 30, 72, 75, 115

PHILADELPHIA MUSEUM OF ART
color photograph: 106.

CITY ART GALLERY, SHEFFIELD
black and white photograph: 34.

NATIONAL GALLERY, WASHINGTON
color photographs: 77, 109.

YALE CENTER FOR BRITISH ART, NEW HAVEN
color photograph: 36
black and white photographs: 42, 107 and page 46.

Concise Bibliography

CATALOGUES

GOWING, Lawrence. *Turner. Imagination and Reality.* Museum of Modern Art. Ed. New York, 1966.

Turner, 1775-1851. Catalogue of Royal Academy. Tate Gallery. London, 1974.

Turner in the British Museum, Drawings ans watercolours. London, 1975.

Turner and the Sublime, by Andrew Wilton, British Museum. London, 1981.

Turner en France. Centre culturel du Marais. Paris, 1981.

CHAPTER I

Joseph Mallord William Turner was the son of a barber and wigmaker. His father's shop was located in Covent Garden, a district famous for its sprawling flower and garden market, which Turner would never forget, and its theater (founded in 1732, twice destroyed by fire, known today as the Royal Opera House). Given the crucial importance of visual impressions during childhood—especially if the individual turns out to be a painter—it is interesting to note that Turner's first experience of the world was near a colorful market and a theater, where lighting effects and perspective joined forces to heighten the joys, fears, and follies of human passion.

The household in which he grew up was far from tranquil. Turner's emotionally unbalanced mother was subject, first to sudden changes in mood, then, as her condition worsened, to violent tantrums. Her mind gave way to what would probably be diagnosed today as schizophrenia. Born Mary Marshall, she was the daughter of a butcher who was pleased with his business and investments. Curiously, Turner inherited the names of his maternal grandfather, to which that of his father was added. We know little about the elder Turner; apparently he assumed the roles of both father and mother. He was a loving and devoted parent who always placed great confidence in his son. A little girl, Mary Ann, was born when Joseph was three. But the child succumbed to the burden of an unfortunate heredity or a sickly constitution; she fell gravely ill and died at the age of eight. As the years wore on, his mother's condition deteriorated and in 1800 she was admitted to Bethlem Hospital, London's insane asylum. No further reference was made to her; her name was never mentioned again. It is believed that she remained in the asylum until 1804, but the exact date of her death has yet to be confirmed. When young Turner was sent away to his mother's family in Margate to recover from an illness, he sketched the main street, the harbor, the cliffs at Birchington, and St. John's church. He must have come away from Margate with lasting memories, for it was here that he returned at the end of his life. The year his sister was taken ill, he was once again sent away, this time to his mother's brother, a butcher who lived in Brentford, on the banks of the Thames. Turner was deeply impressed by what he saw during his stay in Middlesex. He discovered Twickenham and its villas, while across the river he could see Hampton Court, with its immense lawns and venerable trees. He accompanied his hosts when they moved to Sunningwell, on the outskirts of Oxford. There was much to beckon the lad outdoors: an ancient city, the gently rolling hills all around, and once again the Thames. He was fascinated by the endless procession of ships that glided along the bustling river. He spent his time "tormenting the watermen, beseeching them to let him crouch anywhere in the bows, quiet as a log, so that he might get floated down there among the ships, and round and round the ships, and by the ships, and under the ships, staring and clambering;—these the only quite beautiful things he can see in all the world, except the sky; but these, when the sun is on their sails, filling or falling, endlessly disordered by sway of tide and stress of anchorage, beautiful unspeakably; . . ."(Ruskin).

(1) "The more one studies Cozens, the more one is convinced that his romantic essentialism was a justifiable choice—one that was a revelation to Turner and Girtin as they copied watercolors at Dr. Monro's, where Cozens had spent his last years. It was there that they discovered the style and spirit of the great landscape artist. In light of John R. Cozens's essentialism (that is, his anti-realism), the homage the Constable paid him reveals as much about one as the other, 'Cozens is all poetry—the greatest genius that ever touched landscape painting.' Riveted as Constable's eyes were to the minutiae of reality, Cozens helped him understand that what really counted was an individual confronting space, experiencing its vastness, silence, and solemnity, then conveying that solitary experience to others. With the two Cozens, perhaps we need to take the definition of landscape as 'a state of mind' a step further and round it out with another: reality is an optical illusion."

CHAPTER II

(1) Turner's Technique

Turner's technique piqued the curiosity of his contemporaries. Painters at the time were eager to learn about devices, formulas, and tricks of the trade that they, in turn, might use to advantage. Even the venerable Academician, Joseph Farington, went to make inquiries at the artist's studio. Turner, he notes in his diary, "paints on an absorbing ground prepared by Grandi [Sebastian Grandi, his assistant] and afterwards pumissed by himself. It absorbs the oil even at the fourth time of painting over. When finished it requires three or four times going over with mastic varnish to make the colours bear out. He uses no oil but Linseed oil. By this process he thinks he gets air and avoids any *horny* appearance" (quoted in Finberg). A fortnight later, Farington found himself in Turner's studio once again, and he describes, with some surprise, the limited number of pigments the painter used: "White, Yellow Oker, Raw and burnt terra di Sienna, Venetian red, Vermilion, Umber, prussian blue, blue black, Ultra-marine. Linseed oil only" (quoted in Finberg).

John Walker points out in his study of Turner that "it was a sound procedure, and these early paintings have, on the whole, lasted better than his later works." Subsequent paintings, with which Turner apparently took fewer precautions, deteriorated more easily and today are a source of serious concern, especially among curators at the Tate Gallery.

But Farington's interest in the budding artist's methods was not enough to tip the scales in his favor, and his opinion of Turner was consistent with that expressed by *True Briton* in 1802: "much too indeterminate and wild." "Turner strives for singularity and the sublime but has not the strength to perform what he undertakes. His pictures have much merit, but want the scientific knowledge and the Academick truth of Poussin, when he attempts the highest style, and in his shipping scenes he has not the taste and dexterity of pencilling which are found in such excellence in the Dutch and Flemish masters" (quoted in Finberg).

(2) Turner's friendly relations with Jacques Philippe de Loutherbourg—painter, designer of stage sets, favorite scenery–painter of the great actor David Garrick—resulted in greater familiarity with the problems of optical effects. The Alsatian–born expatriate was the inventor of the *Eidophusikon* (1781), a panoramic show of moving scenery and light. His passion for theatrical illusions helped establish the vogue for visual effects and contrivances in the eighteenth century. Given the dearth of power sources at the time, the stage sets of this period were phenomenally daring. Written descriptions cannot do justice to the wonderful surprise effects that audiences came to expect, and got. The *camera obscura* so dear to Poussin was being used in studios everywhere. Gainsborough availed himself of a kind of magic lantern. And no discerning and self–respecting art lover would take strolls in the countryside without his Claude Glass, a small, dark, convex hand mirror that reduced the size of the reflected landscapes and subdued colors so that they might be seen solely in terms of light and shade.

CHAPTER III

(1) The Liber Studiorum

Turner got the idea for the Liber Studiorum from William Frederick Wells, according to Clara Wells, his daughter. "He [Wells] was constantly urging Turner to undertake a work on the plan of the Liber Veritatis," she writes in a letter dated July 27, 1853. "I remember over and over again hearing him say—'For your own credit's sake, Turner, you ought to give a work to the public which will do you justice.' Turner placed implicit confidence in my father's judgment, but he required much and long continued spurring before he could be urged to undertake Liber Studiorum."

Turner must have found the model tempting indeed, for it carried with it the immense prestige of Claude Lorrain. At the age of thirty–five, Claude had already achieved international renown, and it was not long before forgeries of his work began to surface. Therefore, in 1635 he decided to copy all of his paintings in a sketchbook, recording the name of the person who commissioned the work and, after 1647, the date. A number of notable figures were anxious to secure this set of marvelous drawings. Cardinal d'Estrées, the French ambassador to the Vatican, tried to negotiate it for Louis XIV. It was finally acquired by the second Duke of Devonshire. In 1950 the British government accepted it as probate settlement, and it was handed over to the British Museum. After being taken apart, restored, and reassembled, the Liber Veritatis was exhibited in its entirety for the first time in 1977 by the museum's Department of Prints and Drawings.

Turner probably never saw the original. His idea for the Liber Studiorum was based on the engravings of the 1777 edition brought out by Richard Earlom. In order to more closely approximate his illustrious and much–admired model, Turner first thought of adopting Claude's own combination of etching and mezzotinting, then switched procedures. The results were, admittedly, mediocre. His work with these line engravings and etchings dragged on for twelve years (1807–1819), despite the collaboration of Charles Turner and other engravers. Turner himself had to call the project to a halt before it could be completed. As Turner saw it, the Liber Studiorum was first and foremost a compendium of landscapes, but it was also intended to be a showcase for his multifaceted talent. In the best academic tradition, he subdivided the plates into logical, structured categories: "Landscape Compositions, viz. Historical, Mountainous Pastoral, Marine, and Architecture." The original plan called for a total of one hundred plates. On publication, however, the Liber Studiorum. ". . . constituted fourteen parts in all; each contained five plates, labelled with initial letters for each of the landscape types Turner specified in the title; in practice these were varied somewhat, and he frequently used the designation 'EP' meaning, probably, 'Epic' or 'Elevated Pastoral' in place of one or other of the regular categories" (Wilton).

The engravings were uneven in quality, but at least the collection made his work more available to the public at large. In 1820, Turner himself brought out another series of engravings known as the Little Liber, or Sequel to the Liber Studiorum. Unlike the plates of its predecessor, those in the Little Liber turned out to be exceptionally fine. Although it strayed from the original Liber in spirit, its violent contrasts and powerful, dramatic highlighting took up where the last plates of the Liber Studiorum left off (as in Stonehenge). In spite of its technical virtues, however, the Little Liber was not widely circulated.

CHAPTER IV

(1) The Grand Tour was much more than a cultural institution. It was a kind of apprenticeship in life, a learning by experience that enjoyed peak popularity around the second half of the eighteenth century. By 1819, its heyday was history, and its spirit was no longer the same. This exercise in self–edification, as much in vogue among scented (but filthy) aristocrats as among the finicky (but impressionable) middle class, included a fervent quest for the works of art of classical antiquity. Both ancient and "modern" painting were usually on the agenda. There were huge profits to be reaped from so popular a venture, and agents of all types stepped forward to make the necessary arrangements. The renowned "Consul Smith," in addition to being a diplomat assigned to Venice, was a shrewd businessman who had a virtual monopoly on Canalettos and kept the London market well supplied with his work. The sculptor Harwood responded to the clamor for "antiquities" with marble originals or copies. Gavin Hamilton had the good fortune to stumble upon a large number of busts at Hadrian's Villa and sold most of them to British collectors. The chief beneficiary of the find was Charles Townely, a dilettante born and bred whose thirst for masterpieces was unquenchable. Upon his death, the British Museum purchased almost the entire collection for the fabulous sum of twenty thousand pounds sterling. Guileless tourists often found themselves mired in ticklish transactions, and clergymen from lowly abbots to Monsignors would place their diplomatic finesse at their disposal.

Many veterans of the Grand Tour left written accounts of their travels: the irascible James Boswell; Tobias Smolett; the political exile and notorious rake John Wilkies; and the brothers Beckford, Peter the wise and William the eccentric. In Peter's memoirs we find an exuberant description of how English tourists would converge on their "headquarters," the Piazza di Spagna, where they would quickly fall victim to importunate antique dealers and agents for archaeological excursions, hawking not only a guaranteed number of "discoveries," but a healthy share of "sublime" experiences and "picturesque" mishaps.

(2) Walter Fawkes sent a copy of the exhibition catalogue to Turner. "My dear Sir," he wrote, "the unbought and spontaneous expression of the public opinion respecting my Collection of Water Colour Drawings, decidedly points out to whom this little catalogue should be inscribed. To you, therefore, I dedicate it, first as an act of duty, and secondly as an offering of Friendship; for, be assured, I can never look at it without intensely feeling the delight I have experienced during the greater part of my life from the exertion of your talent and the pleasure of your society. That you may year after year reap an accession of fame and fortune is the anxious wish of your sincere friend, Walter Fawkes." Turner replied by decorating a copy of the same catalogue with some watercolors and sending it to Fawkes. The family has held on to it ever since, for it recalls the hospitality they extended to Turner at Farnley Hall.

CHAPTER V

(1) Lord Egremont's estate, with its park and man–made lake, was a marvel of landscape design. Every turn brought fresh surprises and delights. The overall concept was to contrast order and freedom, to counterbalance mathematical precision with the unexpected. Lord Egremont's father (the Second Earl) not only inherited the family collection, but enlarged it with a number of fine canvases he brought back from his Grand Tour. His son followed his example and was especially partial to the work of modern English painters. Many artists gravitated toward this easygoing eccentric who had inherited his title and a yearly income of over two hundred thousand pounds at the age of twelve. "Petworth," wrote Charles Gréville in his celebrated diary, "looked like an inn in its heyday. People came when convenient and left without warning or farewells." No two men could have been less like than lord Egremont and Turner, yet they remained lifelong friends; Egremont, a gentleman by birth and Turner, the son of a poor barber. Turner's height was a constant source of chagrin to him, and he never went out of his way to make himself more presentable. Nor did he ever manage to correct his cockney accent, a grave defect in the eyes of any well–bred Englishman. Yet, Petworth was Turner's home away from home; Lord Egremont went so far as to set up a studio for him, a rare privilege in those days. The death of Turner's father was a severe blow—Thornbury tells us that he was "never the same man"—though the hospitality extended to him at Petworth eased his sorrow somewhat.

Turner had an odd master–servant relationship with his father. Apparently neither one of these sullen companions in coarseness knew how to show his affection. "Dad never praised me for anything except saving a halfpenny," he once said of the elder Turner, who lived with the artist as his housekeeper and assistant. The three surviving letters he wrote to his frugal father consist of strongly–worded, even curt suggestions or instructions.

(2) "Alas, . . . Sir Thomas followed the coffin of Dawe to the same place. We then were his pallbearers. Who will do the like for me, or when, God only knows how soon; my poor father's death proved a heavy blow upon me, and has been followed by others of the same dark kind. However, it is something to feel that gifted talent can be acknowledged by the many who yesterday waded up to their knees in snow and muck to see the funereal pomp swelled up by the carriages of the great." (letter to George Jones, January 22, 1829).

CHAPTER VI

At the Royal Academy exhibition of 1831, Caligula's Palace and Bridge was displayed next to Salisbury Cathedral from the Meadows by John Constable, a splendid, unassuming painter who had gained prominence at last and been elected a member of the Academy in 1829. Above all Constable loved his native Suffolk; one might go so far as to say that it was his only subject. The fact that those in charge of the exhibition saw fit to hang the two paintings side by side is intriguing because it was intentional; enlightening, because it points up very nicely the differences between their approaches.

Constable spoke the language of Wordsworth's "natural painting," while Turner preferred the dazzling effects of Byronic heroism. Thus, the gap separating his concept of painting from that of Turner's was unmistakable. Yet, Constable was too sensitive and refined a soul not to acknowledge Turner's skillful handling of light effects. Although there is no reason to think that Turner was not on good terms with his colleague, surely he must have realized how much everything his art stood for challenged the deeds (and misdeeds) of "culture," even if this raises the question so astutely put forward by Jean-Jacques Mayoux: "But does that make him all that much 'truer' to nature?"

But all of the values Turner so fiercely defended were already being repudiated. For entirely different reasons, the clique of young pastor Fisher, Constable's patron, took up where Sir George Beaumont had left off. As we all know, such choices and determinations are not based on reason alone; powerful emotions run just beneath the veneer of "sensible" arguments. If we assume that Turner was open to these new theories, or even if he simply had misgivings about them, one wonders about the effect painters like Richard Parkes Bonington and Constable had on his own attempts to throw off the heavy shackles of academic tradition. True, an art that stripped nature clean of sublime associations must have struck Turner as insufferable, but he probably found it enticing nonetheless. The inquisitive painter was always on the lookout for technical secrets, and he had no qualms about borrowing from others in order to perfect his craft. After all, without Constable's example, would Delacroix have repainted the background landscape of The Massacre at Chios before exhibiting it at the Salon of 1824? Without Constable, Delacroix might not have resolved to cross the Channel to get a closer look at this English school that held the promise of fresh approach to the world. He reached London in May, 1825, and tried to locate Turner and Constable, neither of whom, unfortunately, was in the capital at the time.

CHAPTER VII

(1) "I went yesterday to see Mr. Liebricht, an oculist in Albany Street. . . . He is the oculist who discovered the cause of all those outrageous effects which Turner produced in his pictures of later years—those wonderful yellows and distorted forms which his admirers kept on declaring were fresh triumphs of art and genius. The pupil of Turner's eye was in a state of disorder but remediable." A similar explanation has been suggested with respect to the strange, flamelike elongation of human figures in the work of El Greco. This sort of interpretation, however, does not resolve the question of how and why an artist's style evolves as it does. Throwing caution to the winds, some have blithely asserted that Turner simply did not know what he was doing. While it is true that hazy outlines became an increasingly characteristic aspect of his manner, most of his watercolors from the same period have their share of well-defined forms, too. But it is also true that many of his friends were astonished to see how, come varnishing day, Turner would touch up a painting at the last minute, his nose glued to the canvas, never stepping back to assess the effects his changes were making.

(2) "May 3, 1862. My dear Wornum: As the authorities have not thought it proper to register the reserved parcel of Turner's sketchbooks, and have given me no direction about them, and as the grossly obscene drawings contained in them could not be lawfully in any one's possession, I am satisfied that you had no other course than to burn them, both for the sake of Turner's reputation (they having been assuredly drawn under a certain condition of insanity) and for your own peace. And I am glad to be able to bear witness to their destruction, and I herely declare that the parcel of them was undone by me, and all the obscene drawings it contained burnt in my presence in the month of December 1858. [signed] J. Ruskin"